PRAISE FOR *OF TEACHING, LEARNING AND SHERBET LEMONS*

Nina's book is so refreshing — and just like sherbet lemons, it's full of fizz! But don't be fooled by the relaxed style and easy readability. This book is packed with some serious advice and guidance which will be of use to anyone working in a school. Whether you're an experienced head teacher or just starting out as a classroom assistant, you'll find plenty to make you think, to challenge you, to help you, and yes, even to amuse you on those difficult days. The user-friendly layout means it's a useful guidebook for when you're seeking help or inspiration in a specific area, but it's also a book you can read through from start to finish. You won't put it down without being left with some great ideas.

John Kendall, head teacher, Risca Community Comprehensive School

If life is a box of chocolates, as Ian Gilbert reminds us in his foreword to Nina Jackson's *Of Teaching, Learning and Sherbet Lemons*, teachers and learners are bound to bite into some unexpected hazelnuts. We don't need to spit blood. It's a short step from Turkish delight to tyranny, as Edmund found in Narnia.

'Ninja' Jackson is a well-known and much loved educator, learner, teacher and sharer of ideas. Inspiration pours forth from her like a fountain, a chocolate fountain perhaps, and catching the drops and putting them down on paper for us all to share is her aim in this book. The process is a dialogue not a lecture: she wants to hear from us, to improve, to tweak, to learn and learn again.

The book is divided into a series of real-life questions, answered with helpful hints, think-points and resources to share. The sherbet lemon analogy refers to the gains to be had from working your way through to the fizzy centre of an idea or practice. It's hard but utterly worthwhile. Nina discusses tough learning support issues, such as ADD/ADHD, inclusion and dyslexia. Lest this seem a little dry, Nina turns each question into a mouth-watering midget gem by asking apposite questions and suggesting leads and approaches. Difficult colleague? Ways forward are suggested. Issues with a colleague's boring lessons? Try this.

Nina's whole approach is collaborative, civilised and compassionate. Not for her the certainties of 'one size fits all'. She has suggestions not solutions, openings not dead-ends. This book is a celebration of the diversity of 21st century education written by woman who is not wedded to the certainty that someone else is wrong and she is right. As a reader you can pick and mix from Nina's sweet jar and relish the variety of flavours and styles. Nor are they all old-fashioned humbugs-in-a-jar. Nina is up on her apps and down with the digital leaders. What holds it all together is a guiding philosophy of education which has been built on and practised for several

D0781059

generations, as the frequent references to her family members testify. Crucially, these offerings are to be savoured and relished. Nina's sherbet lemons are classics: instantly recognisable, totally distinctive and utterly memorable.

Dr Robert Massey, director of scholars, Bristol Grammar School

This book is packed full of practical advice and stunning resources covering many different issues that teachers, learners and parents face every day. It would make a great reference book for trainee teachers (and those already in the profession) as it provides not only a toolkit for dealing with those challenges that we all face but it also helps us to realise that we are not alone. At its heart is the importance of learning for all – teachers included.

Nina makes the simple but pivotal point that learning how to motivate and engage your learners is essential for great teaching. This is an issue that is right at the heart of every day teaching and learning. She also offers a refreshing approach to holistic education. Teachers are there to encourage all learners to be the best they can be and to develop the whole child. Later on in the book, this idea comes through more strongly with the beautiful phrase, 'the invisible stamp', which sums up what should be every teacher's approach to every learner in their class.

There are some helpful ideas on coping with the reality of inclusion – the SLIM resource is wonderful. It should be printed out and put in every staffroom! And I like the way that dyslexia is seen as a gift and not a disability, if the child is also made aware of their strengths and talents. The chapter on INSETs makes some crucial points about the importance of continuing professional development 'as long as it serves to make us even better at what we do'. The posters and artwork are powerful and meaningful. Just fantastic.

Julia Stevens, organisational development director, Halesowen College

I had the great good fortune of attending, in the 1970s, a primary school blessed with a group of highly innovative teachers for whom the child was very much the centre. The mantra of George Hartley, the head who had recruited them, was that each child had his or her own unique talents and that it was the role of the school to fan these into a flame. The range of talents within the pupil body might be very diverse, but each was to be celebrated as a God-given gift that should be developed, not only for the good of the children themselves but ultimately for society as a whole. The head's vision for his students was ambitious and saw beyond the day when they would leave the school to move on to the local secondary schools. Allied to this was his desire to encourage learners to pursue intellectual lines of enquiry as far as they could take them, using the resources of the school and local library and enthused by the passions of the teachers. The message we, as children, received loud and clear was that learning was meant to be exciting and fun, an exploration of the wonderful world around us and of the ideas of those who had shaped it. There was a good dose of 1970s optimism about all this, but the feeling was palpable that the old, more rigid educational philosophies of the past had been thrown off and more creative approaches to learning embraced.

Hartley would, I feel, have recognised a kindred spirit in Nina Jackson. Her latest book, *Of Teaching, Learning and Sherbet Lemons*, advances an equally pupil-centred and humane view of education, one that, while grounded in academic research and sound pedagogy, is thoroughly imbued with the author's infectious, almost missionary enthusiasm for the process of teaching and learning. The reference in the title to sherbet lemons is not accidental. As Jackson makes clear in her introduction, 'fizz' is what the book is all about and refers to the excitement generated in the best lessons when the learning process suddenly comes alive for the students. Pursuing her metaphor, she talks about breaking through the hard but necessary exterior of the sherbet lemon to access the fizz within, a theme that shapes her whole thesis with its balanced but stimulating emphasis on the need for teachers to recover the motivation that brought them into teaching in the first place.

The book is remarkable for the range of topics it covers. Jackson deals with issues as diverse as pushy parents, dysgraphia, the digital revolution, learning styles and self-harm, as well as the area for which she is perhaps best known, the therapeutic value of music in education. In all, she is keen to engage readers in lively discussion, encouraging us to try the very practical hints she gives and to get back to her with feedback. Her energy and enthusiasm, with the sense she gives of being on the side of teachers overwhelmed by bureaucracy and form-filling, mean that one is swept along by her positive vision of how wonderful the teaching vocation can still be. The book is best read a chapter a day in the first instance, each being a self-contained whole that can be absorbed and reflected on before moving on to the next. After this, it can be treated as a resource to be dipped into as time allows, its value being not only to enthuse the jaded professional but also as a call to action. The question-and-answer format that begins each chapter quickly draws the reader in, the imaginary teacher asking the question always being treated with respect and sensitivity and the dilemmas posed being a compendium of contemporary teaching's hot topics.

There are so many valuable ideas and references here that no one who feels inclined to follow up Jackson's insights will be short of material. What makes the book especially appealing is that she wears her learning lightly, and anyone who has ever been put off by educational jargon when approaching a book of this kind will soon be reassured. Jackson is aware that tired teachers sometimes approach INSET in a mood of terror mingled with boredom, and she is clearly determined to avoid the pitfalls that lurk at every corner for the author straying into this territory. There is a very real sense that she cares about the difficulties teachers face in the classroom and that, not only does she want to help, she also wishes to inspire. I recommend *Of Teaching, Learning and Sherbet Lemons* unreservedly to anyone who feels that their teaching lacks the fizz their students deserve. If you feel you spend all your time sucking a sherbet lemon, only to find that nothing lurks within, Jackson amply fulfils her aim of putting the inspiration back.

Stephen Oliver, principal, Our Lady's Abingdon

Teaching is a profession to be proud of. Every day, as practitioners, we are faced with a wide range of situations which require us to find quick solutions or to think long and hard about finding the best way to support our learners to progress and achieve their full potential. Every day we ask ourselves questions and wonder whether we have done the right thing or are strong enough to carry on! Learning never stops for teachers.

Nina Jackson offers us a book full of those tricky questions that teachers have asked her over the years. Some practical and factual questions but also some delicate and moving ones. Questions about learners with learning differences, like mutism, dyslexia or dysgraphia; learners with mental health issues, self-harming or grieving; learners transitioning from primary to secondary school. Questions about educational theories like assessment for learning, target-setting, feedback and learning styles. Questions about how to use information and learning technology and move into the digital era of teaching. Questions about our teaching career, self-reflection, continuing professional development, becoming a manager or dealing with pushy parents.

With her accessible and humorous style, Nina offers a safe platform from which we can observe a range of tried strategies and possible paths, reflect on the resources available and review our own preferences and motivation, so we can move forward feeling more confident and re-energised, ready to sort out an issue or tackle the next challenge. As teachers try to cram in every last drop of the curriculum, tick every box created for us and complete endless reports, Nina reminds us of our core purpose with learners: feed the heart to feed the brain. She encourages us to break the mould if necessary, to push the boundaries and to try innovative, fun and engaging activities with learners.

The strength of this book comes from the fact that Nina mixes new and recognised pedagogical theories with hands-on practical activities and visual posters for displaying in classrooms or in the staffroom. Technology features throughout the book with useful pointers to websites, creative apps or information and learning technology tips to encourage engagement, learning or reflection. Music is also discussed with passion to demonstrate how it can feature in classrooms and act as a motivator and learning aid for learners.

Teachers always want to be the best they can be for their students, and Nina reignites our passion for teaching so we can continue to change people's lives through education. If we can also share best practice with colleagues to reassure ourselves that we are not alone in tackling these multifaceted issues, we will benefit endlessly both on a professional and personal level. Nina Jackson, the Ninja, reminds us of the many reasons why we decided to become teachers and engages us in a thought-provoking dialogue.

This is a book to keep handy for years to come as its structure allows us to dip in and out of it easily. As our classes change and we meet new students, all with very individual learning needs, we might find ourselves asking for Nina's honest advice again and again, safe in her embrace (*cwtch*) and ready for the bumpy but exciting ride of our teaching career!

Dr Barbara Van der Eecken, associate director for quality,
Birmingham Metropolitan College

Of

TEACHING, LEARNING

and

SHERBET LEMONS

NINA JACKSON

edited by Ian Gilbert

PAPL DISCARDED

A COMPENDIUM OF CAREFUL ADVICE FOR TEACHERS

 Independent Thinking Press

First published by

Independent Thinking Press
Crown Buildings, Bancyfelin, Carmarthen, Wales, SA33 5ND, UK
www.independentthinkingpress.com

Independent Thinking Press is an imprint of Crown House Publishing Ltd.

© Nina Jackson 2015

The right of Nina Jackson to be identified as the author of this work has been asserted by her in accordance with the Copyright, Designs and Patents Act 1988.

Illustrations © Paul Wrangles 2015

The right of Paul Wrangles to be identified as the illustrator of this work has been asserted by him in accordance with the Copyright, Designs and Patents Act 1988.

First published 2015.

All rights reserved. Except as permitted under current legislation no part of this work may be photocopied (except pages 9, 17, 26, 31, 46, 51, 57, 62, 67, 73, 81, 93, 99, 106, 109, 114, 120, 127, 133, 140, 146, 153, 160, 164, 176, 182, 190, 196, 204, 212, 218, 223) stored in a retrieval system, published, performed in public, adapted, broadcast, transmitted, recorded or reproduced in any form or by any means, without the prior permission of the copyright owners. Enquiries should be addressed to Independent Thinking Press.

Independent Thinking Press has no responsibility for the persistence or accuracy of URLs for external or third-party websites referred to in this publication, and does not guarantee that any content on such websites is, or will remain, accurate or appropriate.

The letter on page 42–43 has been used with kind permission of the Loder family. The resource on page 46 has been used with permission of Olivia Gilbert. The list on pages 216–217 and the resource on page 218 are used with permission of Mark Anderson.

Quotes from Ofsted documents used in this publication have been approved under an Open Government Licence. Please visit http://www.nationalarchives.gov.uk/doc/open-government-licence/version/3/.

Mind Maps™ is a trademark of the Buzan Organisation.

British Library Cataloguing-in-Publication Data
A catalogue entry for this book is available
from the British Library.

Print ISBN 978-1-78135-134-5
Mobi ISBN 978-1-78135-202-1
ePub ISBN 978-1-78135-203-8
ePDF ISBN 978-1-78135-204-5

Edited by Ian Gilbert

Printed and bound in the UK by
Gomer Press, Llandysul, Ceredigion

For Tadcu (Grandad) – Diolch

FOREWORD

Now, don't get me wrong, I'm all for teacher training. There are many perfectly satisfactory teachers out there who started off not knowing *Of Teaching, Learning and Sherbet Lemons* and who now get the job done, day in, day out, and it's their training that got them to that point. Some people, however, well, they are just born to teach.

Nina is like that.

Think about your own school days. For many people there is one teacher who made it all worthwhile, but what was it that teacher had that the others didn't? I suggest that, like Goldilocks, these great teachers had things 'just right'. Strict but not too strict. Up for a laugh but not out of control. Caring but not soft. Unconditionally supportive but no pushover. Relentlessly optimistic about you but honest enough to tell you when you were heading for a fall. Enough of a teacher to help you learn and enough of a human to make you feel special.

At a time when the teaching profession is being dumbed down by accepting unqualified teachers in front of our neediest classes, combined with a 'what works' hype machine telling us to trust neither our own senses nor our professional judgement, encouraging deeply intuitive teaching from people who genuinely care about children seems rather out of step.

But don't underestimate the Ninja!

An experienced teacher in a number of challenging mainstream and special school settings, Nina has also been involved in teacher training at university level, has a master's in education through her own research on the use of music for learning and motivation, is a growing expert in the use of iPads in the classroom, is regularly asked to speak on issues to do with the health and well-being of both staff and children in our schools, and is in demand across the UK and as far afield as Chile, Ghana and Thailand.

So, when people from all walks of educational life come to her for help and advice she is pretty well-placed to help.

It is this very special spirit of care, intuition, creativity, professionalism and love that drives Nina and that drives this book. Use it to reconnect with what you came into the job for in the first place. Use it to help you out of a tough spot with that difficult child. Or that difficult colleague. Use it to better understand issues around special needs and inclusion. Use it to reassure yourself that what you intuitively feel is the right thing to do may well be the very best thing to do. And use it to put the fizz back into your life and practice as a teacher, as a colleague and as a professional.

After all, if life is a box of chocolates, then teaching and learning is definitely a sherbet lemon.

Ian Gilbert
Hong Kong

ACKNOWLEDGEMENTS

Of Teaching, Learning and Sherbet Lemons would not have come to fruition were it not for the dedication, understanding and overwhelming support of so many people who have worked tirelessly and sympathetically with me to get this book into your hands today.

When a book is published and you see the name of the author and editor on the front, most ordinary folk think that it's all been created by those whose names appear there. Trust me, that's not the case. A book is created by a team of people who sometimes work day and night to meet deadlines, who collaborate to get the message 'just right' and who all pull together to create something they hope will give the reader joy, inspiration and with this book ... allowing you to put the fizz back into teaching and learning.

Ian Gilbert – thank you for editing my work and getting my thinking right in the form of beautiful text and messages for learning. For encouraging and supporting me to just 'be me' – whether it's the Ninja (who continues to move in mysterious ways in teaching and learning) or the Nina Jackson with her academic, intellectual and pedagogical stance. You started something over 20 years ago when you believed in me, and continue to be my mentor, coach and supporter. You have put the fizz back into my thinking on so many occasions that I am beholden to your wisdom and friendship. I couldn't have done it without you. Diolch.

Crown House Publishing and Independent Thinking Press – what a team you are. You are the personification of sherbet lemons at times, and I am so grateful for your time, energy and persistence in keeping me on track – well, sometimes anyway. Special thanks to Caroline Lenton, Beverley Randell and the awesome Tom Fitton for making my text come to life on the pages, and my slight obsession with fonts and visualisations and layouts. Thanks also go to Emma Tuck for her work in copy-editing. You are indeed a patient bunch of professionals. Rosalie Williams for her superb marketing and international connections and for making *Sherbet Lemons* arrive in the hands of so many.

To the Independent Thinking Bubble Team who always have the coffee and tea machine running and for being at the end of the phone when anything needs resolving – in minutes, voilà ... it's done.

To my dear partner, Dic Hamer, who sees my own fizz overflowing on so many occasions and knows when it's time to step away and let me work. Few of us have someone so patient and understanding in times of deadlines, late night typing, always knowing when it's the right time to play jazz and not to play jazz! And yes, I'm a challenging individual at times, but his understanding of the Ninja, always on tour, and with my special peculiar ways – you get me, you tolerate me, you love me and you support me ... thank you.

Olivia Loder, Olivia Gilbert and Mark Anderson, thank you for allowing us to use some of your work in this book.

This book would not be full of sherbet lemons if it wasn't for the mastery of super illustrator and magician of all things 'Hmmm ...' @Sparkyteaching. Thank you for making what was in my head come alive and creating fizzy visualisations, just the way I had imagined them. It is indeed an honour for Sparky and *Sherbet Lemons* to have a beautiful relationship in print. Thanks for being *you* – sparky, enthusiastic, understanding my thinking, making it real and turning the book into a wonderfully illustrated compendium of careful advice for teachers.

Finally, my thanks goes to you, the readers, the educationalists, the mums and dads, the people who want to make teaching and learning right and totally fizzy ... for the children you work with or care for.

Let's decide to be the best we can be – for the children we teach are our future.

For now it's over and out ... but do let me know what you think, won't you?

I'm off to the shops to get some more sherbet lemons ...

Nina Jackson
Craig Cefn Parc

CONTENTS

INTRODUCTION

Do you ever wonder if how you see yourself is not the same as how others see you? Have you ever had the privilege of other people telling you what you're really like? There was me thinking I was Nina, the teaching and learning Ninja moving in 'mysterious ways', but when others told me what the *real* me was like, I was quite shocked. Not in a bad way, but in a 'Is that really how you see me?' way. Wow!

I just wanted to help others as much as I could. Why wouldn't I? I was a Ninja, but a caring one, with fire in my belly and sparkle in my eyes, wanting everything in education to be full of that special fizz that I felt when I was in the classroom. But then a friend described me as 'one of life's givers' and pointed out how many people turn to me, both in the real world and online, for help, ideas, reassurance and support when it comes to the pressing sorts of problems professional teachers have but that they don't feel they can go to their colleagues about. So, rather than a Ninja book with me on the cover in something black and tight-fitting, I've decided this is actually a book about sherbet lemons. Sherbet lemons? I hear you ask, why sherbet lemons?

I've always been rather partial to a sherbet lemon. Not just because of its hard exterior and beautifully shaped lemony looks but also because the real essence of a sherbet lemon is getting to the 'fizz' in the centre. When I was in a really boring lesson at school, I would always reach for a sherbet lemon from the bag I had bought from the tuck shop. Being a rather brilliant secret eater in class, I furtively used the sherbet zing to keep me awake through the direst of lessons.

Of course, getting to the sherbet centre takes a while, you know, and you have to work at it. This ain't no easy come, easy go soft centre! For me, this is what education, schools, teaching and learning are all about. We need the solid exterior – the rigour, the rules, the systems and the structures – to make everything work. Without a hard exterior you're all Dip Dab, and that's not half as much fun. Getting through the hard shell makes going in search of the fizzy centre that much more satisfying, and it is here, at the core of teaching and learning, where the most magical things take place, where the real fizz happens. This is the part that really makes everything worthwhile – the chemical reaction that produces outstanding, innovative and motivational teaching and learning for everyone in our classrooms, not just the few. And fizzy teaching and learning is great. It's exciting, it wakes you up and, boy, does it give you some zing.

However, in any jar of sherbet lemons there is always one that seems to have lost its fizz. It's all hard exterior and no exciting middle. Not so much a sherbet lemon as one of those travel sweets that help pass the time on long, tedious journeys. This book is dedicated to the teachers I've met who feel like they've lost their zing, their fizzle, their buzz. The ones who want things to be better, who genuinely care about their practice, who want to be more than just hard exterior through and through, and who want to find the fizz again. The teachers who want the sherbet back in their sherbet lemons.

So, here we are – *Of Teaching, Learning and Sherbet Lemons*: a compendium of careful advice to help all teachers find and re-find their fizz.

But what gives me the right to write this book, apart from a predilection for sherbet lemons? Well, looking back at my varied and interesting career in classrooms, as well as my experience working with teachers in all sorts of schools around the world, teachers, parents, friends and colleagues have always come to me when they needed someone to listen and give them advice, whether on a personal or professional level. My life to date has been full of wonderful and dreadful experiences – some very wonderful and some very, very dreadful. And each experience has contributed to me being what I like to think is a well-rounded individual, even if I am a little crazy around the edges at times. But you know what they say, 'The cracked ones let in the light'!

That said, I have no magic wand to make things better and I certainly don't have all the answers. In education, no one does, no matter what they claim. What I do have, however, is years of experience, an honesty in approaching whatever it is I do or want to do, and a commitment to help everyone be the best they can be. After all, second best just won't do.

What I've discovered in writing this book is that is is often difficult for teachers to find someone they can approach to help them with their professional questions or queries. We are so much like the child in the class who never wants to ask that burning question because they worry it might make them look silly, even if everyone else is thinking the same thing.

Ridiculous really.

More worrying is that, with all the external pressures on schools and teachers these days, many are concerned that asking their colleagues or superiors some of the questions that are in this book might make them look like they are incapable of doing their job. And then where would they be?

Now, that's really ridiculous.

And what about you? If you asked your head of department or head teacher the sorts of questions about learning and teaching that are in this book would they think you 'weren't quite up to it'?

Of course, it's complete nonsense, but it's a worry for many, many teachers. And this is why *Of Teaching, Learning and Sherbet Lemons* came into being – it's like an impartial, caring, experienced educator not linked to your school and there to offer help without judgement or bias. Here to put the sherbet back into the lemons without blame, guilt or a hidden agenda.

All the queries in this book are genuine questions from genuine teachers working in schools like yours all over the country. Of course, I have left out their names, where they teach and where they are from, but I know you will recognise many of the situations and predicaments that I address.

The answer for each query contains my thoughts as well as some background information. You'll also notice that the answer for each question contains different icons:

 This indicates that there are some things to **THINK** about.

 This suggests some activities or strategies to **TRY** for yourself.

 This icon shows where there is a practical **RESOURCE** or additional ideas to help you resolve the query.

I hope you enjoy the book as well as learn a tremendous amount from some of the, let's call them 'tricky and delicate', questions posed by teachers. Let me know if the advice helps you, won't you, and, of course, if you have a friend or colleague in need and they want to ask anything – and I mean anything – then send them my way. I have plenty of sherbet supplies to top up those hard lemon exteriors. And if the sherbet lemons fail then I can always slip into that tight-fitting black number and be the Learning Ninja too – or maybe that's for another book.

1

THE DRAGON DEEP INSIDE

Q THERE IS ONE LITTLE GIRL IN MY CLASS WHO NEVER TALKS EITHER TO ME OR TO HER PEERS. WHAT CAN I DO?

A This is an important question but, in return, I have so many questions for you to consider too:

- Have you seen or heard her talk to anyone else in the school?
- Is she just a 'selective mute' in school?
- Have you spoken to her parents about this problem?
- Do you know if she has an existing condition, such as a speech and communication difficulty (SCD) or speech, language and communication needs (SLCN)? If so, what is the current level of support within the school? Is any medical intervention with a speech and language therapist taking place?
- Has she stopped talking recently or has it always been this way?
- How do you get her to communicate her thoughts, her learning, her thinking and her emotions?
- Is she a happy child? For example, does she smile?
- Does she look sad or is she just shy?
- Does she have difficulty maintaining eye contact?
- Is she reluctant to smile and at times has blank facial expressions?
- Are her body movements often stiff and awkward?
- Is she always alone or does she play with others without speaking to them?

● Have you discussed your concerns with the head teacher or special educational needs coordinator (SENCO)?

When a child doesn't talk at all there may be a developmental delay or they may have a medical condition. However, when a child speaks and understands language, but doesn't speak in certain situations, they might have selective mutism. This is a condition that was once commonly associated with autism but is now recognised as an anxiety disorder. This is why it's essential for you to understand the 'bigger picture' of this child's social behaviours.

Sometimes children displaying the symptoms of selective mutism may just be considered quiet or shy at first. Often a parent or someone else (you in this case) who is familiar with the child will see that they have some or all of the symptoms. A healthcare professional who is experienced with anxiety disorders will be able to diagnose selective mutism. Early diagnosis and treatment can minimise the effects of the disorder, which can in turn reduce further issues later in life.

I will share with you my thinking and possible courses of intervention. However, I must stress that you should consider the questions above and the statements below in order to best help your pupil. There could be a number of underlying problems that are leading to her not talking.

 Please **THINK** about whether your pupil demonstrates any of the following signs and whether there is evidence of any of the issues outlined:

● The child is consistently unable to speak when it comes to certain social situations, like school, even though they are able to speak elsewhere, such as when they are at home and with their immediate family. This can be a vicious circle that leads to further social isolation and withdrawal. This will interfere with the child's educational achievement and social communication. Later on, if left untreated, it will also impact on their occupational achievement.

● A child will need to show signs of not talking for at least a month in order for it to be considered a possible anxiety issue. However, the first month of school does not count since a lot of children are quite shy during this time, so this shyness needs to be ruled out first.

● Take into account that a child who has selective mutism may also have a tendency to worry about things more than other children do.

- A child with selective mutism will be extraordinarily sensitive to noise, crowds and busy situations. They may also fear going into public places like shops, toilets or generally crowded areas.

- The child will have difficulty with both verbal and non-verbal expression, which means that they can be very much in their own little world and may not always hear everything you say.

- A child with selective mutism may have frequent temper tantrums at home. These can often be physical rather than verbal.

- A young child with selective mutism may often cling to their parent or carer. This makes school a difficult place to settle, hence them choosing not to talk. It could also be that, due to anxiety, they are physically unable to talk due to throat spasms.

- Selective mutes may appear to be excessively shy when, in reality, they have a fear of people.

- A child with selective mutism may also have an anxiety disorder such as social phobia, which means they do not play well with their peers.

 I know this all sounds quite frightening but there are avenues you can explore. **TRY** these strategies with the child to see if they help.

STIMULUS FADING

This technique involves taking the child into a controlled environment with someone they trust, and with whom they can easily communicate. Gradually another person is introduced into this 'safe' environment through several small steps over a period of time. This is known as 'sliding in' or simply 'little steps'. Usually it takes a relatively long time for the first two people to be introduced. Nevertheless, through this technique the child learns to communicate in a small group setting. If there is still no talking, then just quietly interact with the child using toys, games, written prompts or just be physically close enough so that they feel safe but not threatened.

DESENSITISATION

This technique enables you to communicate with the child through role play, such as pretend speaking on a phone and via pictures, toys or written messages left randomly in the child's sitting or working areas. This helps them to become mentally prepared to take the next step, which is communicating verbally. Remember, this will be a slow process, but you have to keep at it. A supportive atmosphere is key.

If a child is positively diagnosed with selective mutism, then anxiety therapy may be recommended to treat the disorder. With early intervention and effective therapy, children with selective mutism are able to overcome their anxiety and function in a variety of social situations.

Several types of therapy are effective in treating this anxiety disorder – you might like to try some of them in school. *Play therapy* is an effective therapy choice for children because they tend to be relaxed and less anxious when they are playing. Progress in play therapy then be transitioned into real-life social situations. *Shaping* uses a structured approach to reinforce all efforts by the child to communicate (e.g. gestures, mouthing, whispering) until audible speech is achieved. There is no specific time frame when this might happen.

It's very important that you talk to the other children in the class about the pupil's unwillingness to speak. Stress to them that they should not force her to speak, but encourage them to interact with her as much as they can – for example, through gestures and non-verbal signs.

 On page 9 is a **RESOURCE** you might like to use in your classroom to help the other children understand.

 Another great **RESOURCE** is the website, www.anxietyuk.org.uk – check out the section on selective mutism.

I hope these strategies will help you to support this young lady.

MY DRAGON WILL NOT LET ME ROAR!

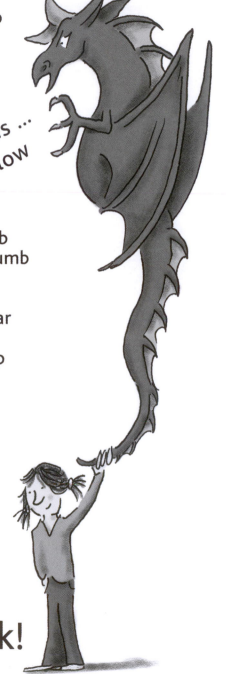

Scared ... afraid ... I cannot speak
My dragon grabs me ... he takes me deep
Inside my body, inside my soul

He stops my words ...
They will not flow

My dragon hides inside my heart
My head, my mouth ... all other parts
My feet, my hands, he makes them numb
Dragon ... stop ... let me speak, not be dumb

I shake and shake and shake some more
When my teacher speaks ... I want to roar
Dragon, dragon, let me speak,
Don't hold my words and make me weep

I'm shy, I'm mute, I am so sad
This dragon in me ... oh so bad
With strength and courage, I will try
To make some friends, be not so shy

So when you ask me out to play
I cannot answer and say 'Yay'...
This dragon in me, he holds me back
But one day ...

watch me ...

I'll fight right back!

Resource from *Of Teaching, Learning and Sherbet Lemons* © Nina Jackson, Paul Wrangles, 2015

2

THE RULES OF ENGAGEMENT

Q HOW DO I REALLY ENGAGE MY STUDENTS IN LEARNING? I AM HAVING PROBLEMS GETTING SOME OF THEM TO GET ON WITH THEIR WORK.

A Learning is a part of everyone's life – it's not just something that happens in the classroom. When you are thinking about engaging students, this means considering their needs from a personal point of view as well as from a learning perspective. Learning how to motivate and engage your learners is one of the most powerful skills you need to embed in your daily teaching and learning routines, but often the question is, how do you do it? How do you ensure that *all* children are engaged? And, the most crucial question, how do you know *when* the students are engaged?

As teachers, our hope is that engaging classroom experiences will serve to enrich the lives of our students who will go on to become articulate, expressive, creative thinkers, who are socially responsible, resilient, resourceful and active citizens in the world. The starting point is to remember that education is about teaching young people not subjects. (The worst case of getting this the wrong way round I've come across was when I met an educationalist who called the learners 'clients'. You'll never hook them in if that's the way you see them! But I'm sure you would never see them as clients.)

When we talk about engaging students in their learning, what we are really talking about is how we go about maximising their inner passion to learn. That inner passion exists in every student, regardless of social, cultural or community background. This means that when we think about and discuss learner engagement, we need to look beyond the student's intellect and see the whole person – the real human being, not the name, date of birth, school entry code number or test scores. Who is the individual behind the data?

Engagement in learning is about providing students with opportunities to be challenged, to be creative. It's about getting their adrenaline going, getting them excited by learning and for learning, and fired up to make progress. The motivation and engagement of each learner should be like an addiction – the more you get excited by something, the more you want it. It's like a child in a sweet shop (yes, I can relate to that!). Is your classroom full of lots of different mouth-watering opportunities for learning, with something for everyone?

Take the use of technology as an example. Digital technology for learning has radically altered the way we communicate and engage with ourselves, our learners, our parents and carers, our communities and the big wide world in which we live. What's more, many young people find these technologies tremendously engaging. How many children do you know, some boys especially, who can be so absorbed working at a computer but would be totally switched off doing exactly the same activity using pen and paper?

Embracing digital technology for learning can help us to transform teaching, but to achieve this teachers have to be flexible, adaptable and adept at making students' learning experiences meaningful, engaging and thought-provoking. Moreover, new technologies mean that we now have new definitions for what it means to be 'literate'. The child who isn't sufficiently 'academic' to be a traditional 'high achiever' may be a whizz when it comes to computer literacy, and if teachers do not give these students opportunities to achieve and attain, then they are not meeting the learning needs of the whole child. If a teacher is apprehensive or scared of digital technology for learning, and unwilling or unable to include it in their lessons, then they are depriving those learners of an engaging learning experience.

Are you ready to spot those students who need a different and enhanced learning experience and, once you've spotted it, use it to your advantage across their learning? And, on top of various forms of literacy, are you actively seeking to help them develop their curiosity, creativity, communication skills and cultivate an attitude that embraces change? Come to think of it, do your lessons develop *your* curiosity, creativity and communication skills? Do *you* embrace change, particularly changes in digital technology?

There are a wide variety of opportunities for engaging learners, especially when combined with a caring and compassionate approach, a personal understanding of the learners' needs and skills, and empathy towards them as individuals. These are all important building blocks in creating a meaningful relationship, the outcome of which will be that the learners can't help but be engaged in your lessons.

 THINK about this question: what does engagement in, and for, learning mean for us as educators?

- Is it in the amount of work they create?
- Is it in the sparkle in their eyes?
- Is it in the way they respond to your questions?
- Is it in the progress they make during lessons?
- Is it in the excitement of learning that may start with you, extrinsically, but then leads to them wanting to learn intrinsically?

One way of looking at your classroom is what I like to call an 'all you can eat learning buffet'. In this learning buffet are copious amounts of different types of learning food which will allow your students to choose what they like to eat, and how much of it, and also the opportunity to come back to the buffet for either more of the same or to try some of the other options available. Knowing that this learning buffet is always on offer in your lessons will hook them in the minute they walk through the door.

 Here are some dishes from the various learning buffets I have laid on for children in the past. **TRY** out some of these!

60 SECOND BIZZ-BUZZ THINKING

Provide a question and give just 60 seconds for discussion. Share ideas from the 60 second buzz. At the end, to tap into the digital learning buzz, consolidate everyone's thoughts through an audio recording, video or interactive mind map. You might want to try these three apps for Android and iOS devices (these are links to the desktop versions):

- SimpleMind: www.simpleapps.eu/simplemind/desktop

- Mindjet: www.mindjet.com/uk/products/mindjet-for-web/
- Popplet: http://popplet.com

There are plenty more apps, but there is also good old paper and pen too which might prove just as exciting for some!

JOT 3 – TOP 10

Using any format – the good old sticky note, a roll of plain wallpaper on the floor, a space on the window or tattoo writing on hands – get the students to jot down three things they learned in the last lesson or three things that they remember doing.

Then get them to collect their top 10 favourite responses from others in the class, so that they can start to work as a team and share each other's thinking. Remember to collect in their responses as they will form part of the learning and thinking process which you can include in the pupils' 'learning portfolios'. These are evidence-based portfolios that you should be keeping in order to track and trace student progress – or, even better, if they manage the portfolio jointly with you. Digital technology can help you here, as both you and the student can gather their learning evidence to share and show personal attainment and achievement. Furthermore, the student can access their learning portfolio at home and add anything they do as enrichment or extended class work to it.

Remember to take some photos of the Jot 3 – Top 10 activity too, so they can refer back to them during their learning journey. For some pupils this can act as a 'thinking hook' – they will be more engaged because they have been part of the process and have enjoyed working collaboratively. Meeting the needs of all learners through a differentiated approach is the key to success: same task, but different ways of producing and recording it (remember that learning buffet!).

MUSIC FOR ENGAGEMENT

The universal language of music is an amazing way to get your pupils engaged from the off. Choose pieces such as 'Let's Get Ready to Rhumble' by PJ & Duncan (aka Ant & Dec) or even 'C'mon Everybody' by Eddie Cochran. The reason songs like these are amazing tools for engagement is all to do with the fact that 'sound waves make brain waves'. This is a combination of beats per minute combined with just the right lyrics. These songs will get your students' hearts pumping, their bodies moving and their brains fired up.[1]

Remember, when you get your own head around the science and practice of using the right music for the right reason at the right time, then you will also have the skills to be able to choose your own tracks. And if you have explained to the students why the right music for the right reason at the right time is being used, then they too will be able to produce their own playlist of tracks for engaged learning in and out of the classroom.

What's even better, and will absolutely guarantee learner engagement, is if they create their own music. You might suggest iPad apps such as GarageBand, Music Studio, LaDiDa, Loop Twister, BeatMaker 2, Rhythm Pad, Impaktor or Launchpad, or you may want you use Audioboom to get students to record their learning onto a channel that you create for your school or individual student log. Audioboom allows you to record short bursts of audio and post it like a blog. Simple, easy and very learner friendly. You can also make it private so that it only gets shared with those that you want to access it.

PICK 'N' MIX - THE VISUAL WAY

A picture can tell a thousand words and conjure amazing creative thinking in some students. When you choose a topic or area of study, try to source some fantastic pictures to share with the class and get them thinking, wondering, discussing or collaborating, or just simply embedding themselves in a different way of looking at something.

---

1 To find out more about my own research on the effect of music on the brain and for learning, take a look at *The Little Book of Music for the Classroom* (Carmarthen: Crown House Publishing, 2009).

Choose some pictures and place them around the class – under the seats or anywhere that is not just in front of them. Get the students to move around and note one, two, three or more things about each image and what they feel, see or think about when they look at it. This gets students talking quickly and making choices about what they like and dislike. Often they unravel their thoughts about why they are drawn to certain images. Make them all different too – not just photographs but puzzle pictures, cartoons, some with quotes and so on.

Once they have collected their thinking, either through note-taking, audio recordings or digital photos, get them to consolidate this in visual form – a 'thinking mosaic' of all their thoughts. This could be done using Wordle or a mind map, lists, their own drawings or doodles. I often use Photo Collage or Moldiv as ways of presenting a visual representation of my own thinking through photos, because to see it is to absorb it!

As well as presenting students with a set of your own questions about the visual stimuli, you may also want to ask them to create their own questions about the pictures. Share these on a 'thinking wall' or simply discuss their ideas. As a teacher, you will be able to come up with 101 other ways of linking the learning with the visualisations. It's another tasty little tit-bit as part of the learning buffet!

STUMPED

Get your students to create a set of questions with the intention of getting the others 'stumped'. This encourages them to own their thinking as they wonder whether or not the other students will be able to solve their mystery, which in turn leads to an increased sense of intrinsic motivation and helps to build a love of learning. Watch the little giggles and inner sense of celebration when the other students try to guess what the question or scenario is all about. This also supports independent learning and thinking because the trickier the question or scenario, the more they want to solve the problem. In addition, it ensures you involve all the students in the learning and give them a voice – leading the learning *their* way. After all, we need to know what makes them excited about learning, as well as giving them different learning buffet experiences. It's all about choice and tantalising learning experiences.

All You Can Learn...
BUFFET MENU
FOOD FOR THOUGHT.

THINGS THAT I LEARN AND WAYS THAT I LEARN

These are my favourite learning buffet engagement tools to help me achieve and attain the best I can.

Resource from *Of Teaching, Learning and Sherbet Lemons* © Nina Jackson, Paul Wrangles, 2015

Use the **RESOURCE** on page 17 for suggested ways of using the learning buffet diary. Use this as a template to think about different activities, tasks and ideas, or as a template for your students to track the different types of learning experiences they prefer.

In each circle they can note what the learning is and how they have chosen to share it, such as pen and paper, audio, video, internet research, group work, listening to and working with others (there are a variety of icons for them to use). This is a good way for you to find out what their preferences are for different types of activities.

Note: ask the learners to complete each box either during a lesson or over a period of time – you decide as a professional. Ensure there is adequate support for children with special educational needs and disabilities (SEND). You may even want to use the resource directly on a digital device, which will really get the students' taste buds excited.

I hope this is helpful and that you'll find new and different ways of engaging your learners.

3

CONCLUSIVE INCLUSIVE

Q SO MANY TEACHERS IN MY SCHOOL TALK ABOUT INCLUSION AND GETTING IT RIGHT, BUT WHEN I LISTEN TO THEM I'M NOT SURE THEY ARE DOING WHAT THEY SAY THEY ARE DOING – BECAUSE OUR RESULTS DON'T REFLECT IT. I'M NOW CONFUSED AND MUDDLED ABOUT INCLUSIVE LEARNING, WHAT IT MEANS AND WHAT I NEED TO DO TO MAKE SURE ALL MY PUPILS HAVE A GREAT LEARNING EXPERIENCE AND MAKE PROGRESS. CAN YOU HELP?

A I like the way you're making the pupils the centre of your question and how you're not only questioning your colleagues but also yourself when it comes to your thoughts on inclusion. This proves to me that you have the learners' interests at the heart of your teaching, which is the first step towards ensuring every child gets the best education they can. Bravo!

Inclusion is the term we give to the belief and practice that all pupils can be taught in mainstream education with their chronologically age-appropriate peers. The idea is that, with the necessary support and services for pupils with learning difficulties or disabilities in place, a general education can be provided in all classrooms. Inclusion is one of many placement options for pupils with individual education plans (IEPs) or those who have an education health care plan (EHCP). We now know that an EHCP has to be in place due to changes with the special educational needs and disabilities provision in schools. Effective inclusive education requires a high level of collaboration among general education and special education staff and a commitment to ensure the services they provide are as seamless as possible. This means that one of the most important aspects of inclusion is that educationalists collaborate, discuss and share the needs of the pupil. Parental involvement is often key to its success. I hope that if your school does not already have in place a structure for collaboration and the sharing of good practice that you might think about setting one up – for example, a professional learning network to support your own professional development (Twitter is a good place for this).

However, there is also a school of thought that inclusive education and learning is not just about including a particular child or group of children with specific needs, but meeting the physical, social, emotional and learning needs of all children so that they all become accepted members of their school community. Inclusion recognises that all children are different but all need to be included. It means that it's not just about this child being gifted and talented or that child having special educational needs, but that we offer *all* children a classroom experience which meets their own individual learning make-up. This is where differentiation meets inclusion. We all need to have different learning experiences to find the best way for us to learn, think and develop as human beings.

Let me share with you what inclusion is and isn't – maybe you'd like to use these definitions with your colleagues too.

INCLUSION IS NOT:

- An afterthought to general classroom planning and delivery.
- About everyone learning in the same way.
- About making pupils conform to traditional learning systems and methods.
- About knocking square pegs into round holes, ever.
- Just about SEND pupils.
- Planning lots of different and individual programmes.
- Pieces of paper and policies that aren't practical and realistic.

INCLUSION IS:

- Celebrating each pupil's individuality.
- Giving each child flexible learning experiences.
- Taking into account the views of others and valuing all contributions.
- Understanding different cultures and communities as well as your own.
- Looking at the needs of the whole school and its community of learners.
- Guaranteeing the basics and fundamentals of good education for all in terms of teaching and learning.
- Reflecting on your practice and understanding the context of your school.
- Knowing and developing effective relationships with each and every pupil.
- Making everyone responsible for the needs of individuals.
- Embracing diversity.
- Differentiation being at the heart of the school and every learning experience.
- Constantly reflecting on classroom practice and making adjustments to the curriculum and planning for learner needs – it's a continuous process.

> An educationally inclusive school is one in which the teaching and learning, achievements, attitudes and well-being of every young person matters.
>
> **Ofsted,** *Evaluating Educational Inclusion:*
> *Guidance for Inspectors and Schools* **(2000)**

As this is an area you are obviously passionate about, consider whether or not you would want to champion effective inclusion in your school and bring everyone on board to collaborate with ideas and practices. You could begin a working party or discussion forum. Present yourself as an 'inclusion champion'. (You don't have to wear a special badge – just move a learning revolution forward!) And remember, you don't need anyone's permission to do this. It's a professional duty that we should all be doing on a daily basis. If you believe in it, do it!

THINK about:

- Ways you can bring everyone on board with you.
- Managing inclusion inclusively by inviting everyone to join your group based on a mission of sharing professional opinions and experiences.
- How to build on personal beliefs and learning visions.
- Managing the inclusive dilemma in teaching and learning.
- How to interpret the context of your school and its current inclusion approach.
- Building learning communities among teachers, parents and pupils.
- Using the SWOT (strengths, weaknesses, opportunities and threats) analysis approach when considering the context of inclusion in your school.

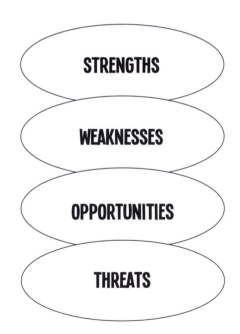

TRY this as a starting point to evaluate current practices and strategies towards inclusion:

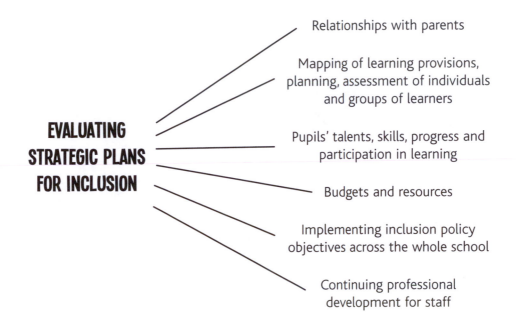

EVALUATING STRATEGIC PLANS FOR INCLUSION

- Relationships with parents
- Mapping of learning provisions, planning, assessment of individuals and groups of learners
- Pupils' talents, skills, progress and participation in learning
- Budgets and resources
- Implementing inclusion policy objectives across the whole school
- Continuing professional development for staff

You may also want to look at the British Council publication, *Inclusion and Diversity in Education*, which remains an outstanding document for understanding inclusion and diversity across the international education system.[1]

---

1   Nargis Rashid, *Inclusion and Diversity in Education: Guidelines for Inclusion and Diversity in Schools* (Madrid: British Council, 2010).

Here is an excellent example of a school improvement cycle for inclusion that you might want to try in your quest for teacher engagement and better understanding:

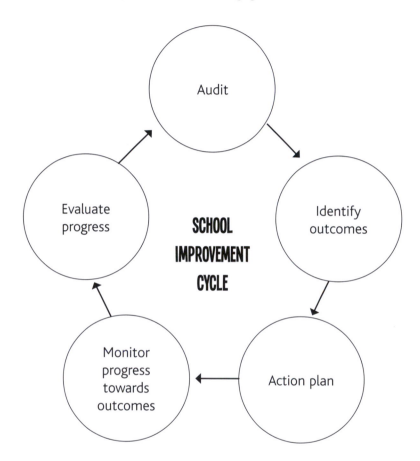

When considering the *audit,* which is the 'Where are we now?' question, take into account the strengths of the school and the positive strands on which you can base the development of the inclusion system, policies and practice.

Moving on to *identifying outcomes* and where you want to be in the short term (about a year) and long term (about three years) in terms of strategic planning and vision, make sure you have a baseline to work from, which will include up-to-date data, and that the criteria for assessing and judging outcomes are realistic. Just remember that data does not a whole person make! It's about *knowing* the pupil and their particular needs, not just the data.

The *action planning* part, working out how you are going to get there, will need to include activities that you can measure against possible outcomes. Ensure you have a team of people in your working group to assist you as the task will be lengthy and will require constant monitoring and evaluating. Your priorities here will most definitely need to be linked to your whole school aims and mission statement.

When you are *monitoring progress* and checking if you are on track, schedule regular review meetings. As much as you can, share the progress to date so that you are fully including all staff in the developments.

By *evaluating progress* and analysing if you have achieved what you set out to achieve, you will be able to come to a conclusion about what has worked and what needs further consideration. Make solid, factual and professional learning recommendations to colleagues to develop your school into a fully inclusive and diverse learning institution.

And that's all there is to it. Good luck!

 You might want to use the **RESOURCE** on page 26 to improve inclusivity in your school.

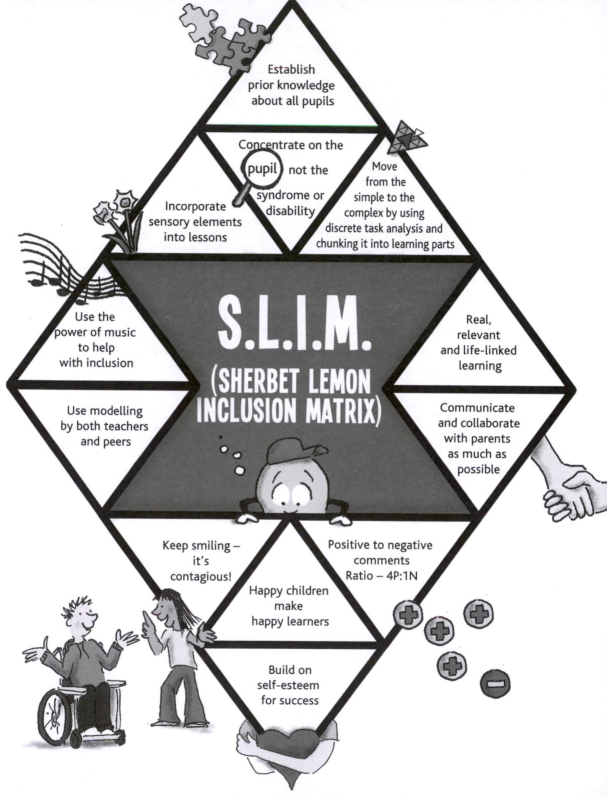

Establish prior knowledge about all pupils

Concentrate on the pupil not the syndrome or disability

Move from the simple to the complex by using discrete task analysis and chunking it into learning parts

Incorporate sensory elements into lessons

S.L.I.M.
(SHERBET LEMON INCLUSION MATRIX)

Use the power of music to help with inclusion

Real, relevant and life-linked learning

Use modelling by both teachers and peers

Communicate and collaborate with parents as much as possible

Keep smiling – it's contagious!

Positive to negative comments Ratio – 4P:1N

Happy children make happy learners

Build on self-esteem for success

Resource from *Of Teaching, Learning and Sherbet Lemons* © Nina Jackson, Paul Wrangles, 2015

4

IS YOUR TOP SOMEONE'S BOTTOM, OR IS SOMEONE'S BOTTOM YOUR TOP?

Q I'M NEW TO TEACHING, BUT I'M AMBITIOUS. WHAT'S THE QUICKEST WAY TO THE TOP?

A I am delighted to hear that you are an ambitious individual. It's good for us all to have personal and professional ambitions as it gives us goals and a sense of purpose. And, oh yes, welcome to the world of teaching! This question makes me wonder what you think 'the top' is in teaching and education. Would it be ...

- Secretary of state for education
- Chief education officer for the local education authority
- Head teacher
- Education adviser
- Head of department
- Head of faculty
- Head of year
- Assistant head teacher
- Deputy head teacher
- Lead learner
- Pedagogy leader

Or is it just simply being an amazing teacher year in year out who has happy, engaged learners who want to come to school because you *are* their teacher? Isn't that being at the top as well?

 With that in mind, have a **THINK** about these aspects of being at the top. Is it:

- Being an outstanding teacher who obviously has an impact on children's learning and overall well-being in school.

- Having a willingness to embrace an ever-changing world of education so that you remain top of your game when it comes to professional learning, development and practice, and therefore being adaptable and flexible to the many and changing needs of your learners?

- Allowing yourself to gain valuable experience from learning the hard way – that is, when things don't go to plan: classes misbehaving, groups of students challenging you, activities and tasks just not working out as you had planned or even one of those 'Oh my gosh, why am I a teacher?' days? (In fact, those are the best types of learning days, when you've got over the shock of things not going to plan and you're having a stiff G&T with ice and a slice to calm you down, and only then can you evaluate what worked, what didn't work and why, to your eyes, the top was never in sight.)

- Those times where you were right on top of your game, with a thirst to try new ideas and embrace change in a learning environment, thinking up new ways to engage and challenge your students?

- When you ask the students themselves what they thought of your lesson and you learn from them honestly and openly about what worked and what didn't? You will gain a tremendous amount of respect as a new teacher if you are willing to engage with the students about their learning in this way.

Whatever your top is in teaching, in my experience there is no supersonic route to getting there, but there is a need to combine knowing what you want with being outstanding where you are at the current time. There are teachers who have been excellent classroom teachers for over 40 years and have had a massive impact on the children they have taught. There are young ambitious individuals, like yourself, who have attained a head teacher position in a short space of time and do extremely well. And there are those who, when they get there, wish they hadn't due to the pressure, stress and anxiety that go with the job.

Sometimes it's a question of perspective, so getting to the top, wherever that may be, can actually feel as if you're on the bottom again. (You know the moment when you're walking up a hill and you think you see the top, only to get there and see another higher point ahead of you. And then you discover you don't have the special equipment to climb those higher slopes.) The Buddha once said that the way to happiness is to learn to want what you have and not to want what you don't have. This is 'the acceptance of reality', and I view it as a cornerstone of mental health, contentment, inner security and peace of mind. And if you have these things, where else are you but at the top?

In order to help you understand where your top is in relation to teaching, however, it's a good thing to set yourself a mini plan. Remember, your ambitious journey to get to the top quickly can be lonely and rocky, especially if you alienate your colleagues on the way. As a wise man once said, 'If you burn all your bridges, eventually no one will be able to reach you.'

And if you're a young aspiring teacher looking to advance your career, you should be aware that there are various reports of young teachers, often under the age of 30, who have been 'fast-tracked' to head teacher jobs, especially in schools in special measures because no one else wants those jobs, who have subsequently struggled. Ordinarily, it takes 18 years, on average, to become a head teacher.[1]

 In order to plan your quickest way to the top, why don't you **TRY** thinking and planning using the following tips:

- Become the best teacher you can be for the children you teach first of all. That way you will have credibility as an outstanding practitioner and be able to coach, mentor and network with similar like-minded professionals.

- It doesn't matter how outstanding we are, there is always room for improvement and trying new things. As Hywel Roberts, friend, colleague, outstanding practitioner and author of *Oops!*[2] has always told me, 'We are only as good as our last lesson and its impact on the young people in it.'

---

1 PricewaterhouseCoopers LLP, *Independent Study into School Leadership* (January 2007). Ref: RB818. Available at: http://webarchive.nationalarchives.gov.uk/20130401151715/http://www.education.gov.uk/publications/eOrderingDownload/RB818.pdf.

2 Hywel Roberts, *Oops! Helping Children Learn Accidentally* (Carmarthen: Independent Thinking Press, 2012).

- Consider asking one of your senior managers to be your coach or mentor so that you can set yourself targets and have an experienced professional to offer you support and guidance.

- Set up collaborative learning networks in your school so that you can really test out your leadership potential – put learning at the core of your ambition, not just your career. This will gain you much credibility and respect. If you are seen to be moving the learning and teaching forward in the school – under your own ambition – and standards of learning and teaching are on the rise, then this will be an opportunity to celebrate innovations in teaching that you have helped make happen.

- Take responsibility for your own professional learning outside school. Read relevant and stimulating literature and research articles, and get on to Twitter. You will see in this book that I have recommended some great educationalists for you to follow, and this will also get you involved in @ukedchat and other online teaching forums.

- Create a professional learning plan for yourself that shows your objectives for promotion and sets out some of the areas where you might want to specialise.

Finally, take a deep breath and ask yourself what it is that you really want. Is it the status of being at the top, wherever that may be, or is your top someone else's bottom?

 There's a **RESOURCE** on page 31 you might like to use as your planning document.

I will leave you with something which may bring a smile to your face. Richard Branson once said: 'Believe in yourself and back yourself to come out on top. A fulfilling career is waiting for those brave enough to find it' – wherever your top may be.

PERSONAL PROFESSIONAL AMBITION PLAN

 A Where am I now?

 B Where do I want to get to?

 ? Why do I want to get there?

 How am I going to get there?

What do I need to do? Timescale?

 What or whose support will I need?

Resource from *Of Teaching, Learning and Sherbet Lemons* © Nina Jackson, Paul Wrangles, 2015

5

DYSLEXIA – A GIFT, A CURSE AND A LEARNING DIFFERENCE

Q I TEACH A NUMBER OF PUPILS IN DIFFERENT CLASSES THAT I HAVE BEEN TOLD ARE DYSLEXIC. SOME ARE IN MIXED ABILITY CLASSES AND SOME ARE IN SPECIAL NEEDS CLASSES. I HAVE NOT RECEIVED ANY TRAINING SO I'M WONDERING HOW BEST I CAN SUPPORT THESE LEARNERS. ANY ADVICE?

A Let me begin by sharing with you some statistics. The British Dyslexia Association have reported that on average over 10% of the British population are dyslexic, 4% severely so. These statistics are only based on reported cases – there are many more people who live their lives not knowing they have dyslexia. Lots of us, teachers included, do not fully understand what dyslexia is and are not sure how to support children with it. In many cases, it's not an obvious difficulty and it can be hidden.

Many dyslexics overcome the barriers of their condition and go on to become brilliant and gifted individuals, often impacting positively on the lives of others. Steven Spielberg, Walt Disney, Steve Jobs, Theo Paphitis, Henry Winkler (The Fonz), Pablo Picasso, Cath Kidston and Roberto Bolaño are all dyslexic but extremely talented in their fields. I wonder how many of your pupils would even know that these people are dyslexic?

In order to support your students, here is a brief summary of what dyslexia is and what it most certainly is not:

● Dyslexia is *not* a disability.

- Dyslexia can be a gift, *if* the person is aware of their many strengths and talents. But being dyslexic does not a gifted person make. Sometimes their skills need to be revealed, as they can be troubled by what they can't do rather than what they can.

- The average person more often than not thinks that dyslexia leads to problems with reading, writing, spelling and maths, and many associate it only with word and letter reversals. But it is much more than this.

- Many people see dyslexia as a form of learning disability, but it is only a disability when a young person is unable to develop skills and strategies to get past the problems it throws up or lets it get in the way of other learning tasks and activities.

As well as providing support for pupils with dyslexia, we need to consider how to help them develop their individual coping mechanisms, so they can find various avenues of achievement and attainment that match their strengths. The key is not to focus on what they can't do but to show them what they can do with the many learning skills they have.

Ronald Davies, co-author of *The Gift of Dyslexia*,[1] tells how he was once a guest on a television show and was asked about the 'positive' side of dyslexia. Apart from listing more than a dozen famous dyslexic people, the TV host commented that it was amazing, despite having dyslexia, that these people were geniuses. Davies suggests she rather missed the point. It was *because* of their dyslexia that their genius flourished!

People with dyslexia do not all develop the same gifts or, of course, all become geniuses, but it is useful to see the mental functioning that causes dyslexia as a gift in the truest sense. It is a natural part of us that is unique to the individual and, in turn, can serve to make that person very special indeed.

Here are some descriptions of dyslexia I have come across, in particular on the British Dyslexia Association (BDA) website.[2]

- Dyslexic people can utilise the brain's ability to alter and create perceptions in different ways.

- Dyslexic people are highly aware of their environment.

---

1   Ronald D. Davies and Eldon M. Brown, *The Gift of Dyslexia: Why Some of the Brightest People Can't Read and How They Can Learn* (New York: J. P. Tarcher/Penguin Putnam, 2010).

2   See http://www.bdadyslexia.org.uk/educator/what-are-specific-learning-difficulties.

- Curiosity is far more prevalent in dyslexic people than in the average person (although I am still not convinced that when we talk about 'average' people that this is a fair description of any human being!).
- Dyslexic people often think mainly in pictures, not in words.
- Dyslexic people can be highly intuitive and insightful individuals.
- Dyslexic people regularly use all their senses and think and perceive in a multidimensional way.
- Dyslexic people can experience thought as reality, as if their internal thinking is real in every way.
- Dyslexic people can have the most amazing, vivid imaginations.

It's important that these gifts are not suppressed, invalidated or destroyed by parents, teachers or others in the 'normal' school setting. If the person with dyslexia can get through their early years intact, then the result is often that we see higher levels of intelligence and extraordinary creative abilities. From these, the true gift of dyslexia can emerge. All of which means that it's our job as educationalists to direct these wonderful, creative people on the right learning highway for them.

THE LEARNING DIFFERENCE

Acknowledging that dyslexia is a 'specific learning difference' will help you to focus on how your lessons are planned, how you create your resources and the way in which the teachers in your school support children with dyslexia through focused practice and an inclusive ethos of learning. Dyslexia-friendly schools identify what is the right thing to do to enhance the effectiveness of learning for all.

Understanding the needs of all learners is paramount for engagement and motivation in learning, so don't wait for a pupil to receive a formal diagnosis of dyslexia. Address the issues head on and look at early intervention for 'learning needs' rather than 'labelled needs'. But then this is what good teachers do, isn't it?

The problems of dyslexia tend to arise most often in the acquisition and application of basic skills. Dyslexic pupils are as good, if not better, at many things their peers do – that is, until they need to write it down. Problems tend to occur in mainstream classrooms in areas such as the speed of processing information, short-term memory, sequencing and occasionally weaknesses in auditory and perceptual skills.

 THINK about whether you have spotted any of these differences in your students:

- Can be a little 'awkward' with tasks at times and occasionally seem to get things in the wrong order. Let's not call it clumsy, though, because it's not – it's just the way their brains are processing what needs to be done.

- Do very well in the arts – drama, music, art – and often are very competent orally.

- Have amazing thinking patterns which are extremely creative but have difficulty with writing.

- Sometimes choose or want to be on their own and can seem isolated and introverted, which is often due to anxiety about writing their thoughts down. They are usually quite happy to converse orally so they can share their thinking that way instead.

- Act as the class comedian, which is often a mask to cover up their anxiety about writing and not being able to fulfil academic requirements (especially boys – I'm not being sexist here, it's a fact!).

- Find memorising lists and specific processes a problem, but can do one thing at a time really well.

- When verbal instructions are given too quickly they can have a 'glazed' look, which often means that they are not processing the information rapidly enough. So, slow it down!

- They can get extremely tired during the afternoon because, after a morning of extensive learning, they have had to put so much effort into what they have done that they are physically and mentally switched off. It's not that they are choosing the off switch button, but it's because their brains really can't work any more. Get some practical and creative activities in place for them during the afternoons.

- They are often picked on or bullied, especially if they are withdrawn from some lessons for 'extra help' or 'support', which lets the other learners know that they are not quite the same as them. Let's make sure we get the inclusion right here.

Keep your eyes peeled for these signs in the early years, primary and secondary phases.

EARLY YEARS DIFFERENCES:

- Some signs of not paying attention.
- Issues with kicking, catching or throwing a ball as well as hopping or skipping.
- Delayed speech development.
- Not always able to clap in time.
- Find learning nursery rhymes or the names of common objects like table, chair, etc. difficult.
- Love being read to, but show no interest in letters or words themselves.
- Struggle with traditional phonics approaches to reading.
- Difficulties with putting shoes on the correct feet or getting dressed efficiently.

PRIMARY SCHOOL DIFFERENCES:

- Problems tying shoe laces (try the Velcro approach!).
- Short-term memory issues.
- Written work might be very messy, which could lead to some dysgraphia issues later on if not helped in the early stages.
- Confusion with certain letters (e.g. b and d, p and q, w and m) resulting in some unusual spelling and pronunciation.
- Reading difficulties (although not all dyslexic children have these). Look out especially for hesitant or laboured reading, omitted lines or repetition of the same phrase, muddling of words (e.g. 'no' and 'on', 'for' and 'off', 'was' and 'saw'), struggling with multisyllabic words and problems with understanding what it is they have read. (I once heard a child saying 'amblumbunce', which is easily

understood by adults as 'ambulance', but be careful not to ridicule the pupil. They will surprise you in so many other ways with their creativity, artistic concepts and being alert and bright – if they are stimulated correctly.)

SECONDARY SCHOOL DIFFERENCES:

Dyslexic students will continue to experience some of the same difficulties as in primary school, but they may also confuse places, dates and times. Additional cognitive and emotional developmental issues could include:

- Getting tied up with words and having difficulty in planning written responses, especially essays.
- Poor confidence and self-esteem.
- Becoming extremely anxious and stressed during testing and examinations – this is because they are often unable to share their thinking processes.
- Attendance can be erratic and exams are often missed. This is sometimes treated as a behaviour issue, when in reality we should be addressing the student's personal learning needs.
- Forgetting their books or struggling to understand a timetable can be very traumatic in secondary school.

TRY some of these strategies with your students, and raise awareness so that your school can become a truly dyslexia-friendly school:

- Always explain things in a variety of different ways, repeating them if necessary.
- Use two colours to mark work, one for content and one for spelling/presentation.
- Correct only spellings that they have been specifically taught.
- Create word banks to support dyslexic learners.
- Set high expectations for intellectual understanding and reasonable ones for written responses.
- When marking work, put yourself in the position of the pupil – try to understand the problems they may have with writing letters (e.g. inside out and back to front).

- Give students a chance to explain and describe their thinking to you orally where possible. You could also get them to record their responses using apps such as Dragon Dictate and Audioboom.

- Most iPads now have the function to allow students to record their responses orally and the app will generate written text (but only if you have the microphone icon built into the iPad and it is used as part of the keyboard functions rather than typed text).

- Be aware of tiredness and fatigue – dyslexic children need to work much harder than others and can become physically and mentally drained, especially in the afternoons.

- Have 'sink in' time – be slow and deliberate with your instructions, allowing time for understanding to be assimilated, and then get them to explain it back to you.

- Use as many multisensory learning methods as you can so that information is most effectively absorbed and stored through all the senses.

- Give constructive praise and support for learning. Remember the four-to-one ratio of praise to criticism.

- Continually give guidance on tackling tasks systematically.

- Dyslexic learners can shine through oral work, so show an interest in their abilities and talents – feed the heart to encourage the brain.

DOs AND DON'Ts
(OR, RATHER, DEFINITELY DO AND DON'T EVEN GO THERE)

- Do use a board or writing area for reminders, but don't use it for lengthy pieces of written work.

- Don't ever keep a child back at breaktime to finish copying down any sort of work if they are dyslexic.

- Do make your writing large, clear and well-spaced. If you are marking a pupil's handwriting, then yours needs to be legible and clear too.

- Do allow plenty of time for children to read from a board, projector, TV, etc. or get them to take photographs of what you are sharing. This is all part of moving and learning in the digital age.

- Do think about dividing a board into different coloured sections to ease place findings.

- Do think about a photocopied or digitally shared transcript of the work.

- Don't ask dyslexic pupils to read aloud unless they are comfortable with this.

- Don't overload pupils with instructions.

- Don't give pupils lengthy facts to remember in a short space of time.

- Don't expect the same quantity of written work as you do from other pupils.

- Don't ever shout at a dyslexic child when they lose or forget things.

 TRY this: ask your dyslexic learners what you can do to make their learning experience better. Remember, pupil voice and learner relationships are your allies. Knowing your students inside out is the key to effective, interesting and thought-provoking learning relationships.

Here are what some students have said about what they would like teachers to do in order to support their learning:

- Talk slowly, plainly and clearly.

- Give us more time to respond to written tasks.

- Explain instructions and check that we understand.

- Watch us and help us with spellings, maybe in the margins.

- Give us your full attention when we are trying to explain our thinking to you.

- Give us hand-outs to summarise the learning or photos on a digital device.

- Mark our work tidily so we can understand your writing.

- Use dark colours – and give clear, helpful comments.

- Judge the work on its content not always on the spelling.

- Please don't shout at us if we forget things.

- Please be patient with us.

- Please look after us the best you can, that's all we want.

And here is something extra special to share with you. Earlier, I described the importance of empowering young people to share with teachers the help and support they need and want, and for us, their teachers, to empower students to be skilled and confident in their learning spaces. Here is a very short but powerful story.

THE TWO OLIVIAs – A WORLD APART AND YET THE SAME IN SO MANY WAYS

They possess beauty and dignity and are determined young women, and they both have a special gift as well as a learning difference.

Olivia Loder attends Moon Hall College, a specialist dyslexia school, one of only four in the UK. She felt so strongly about the lack of teacher expertise and support in mainstream schools that she wrote an extremely powerful letter to Michael Gove, the then secretary of state for education, and received a response from him.

She has also been working with Henry Winkler (aka The Fonz) to raise the profile of dyslexia. Her journey has only just begun, so if you would like to offer your support to Olivia, please follow her on Twitter: @LoderOlivia. You might also like to follow her dad, Tim Loder (@LoderTim), who is working closely with the British Dyslexia Association and other parents to champion dyslexia. Olivia's journey has also meant she was chosen from hundreds of children who suggested an app to help learners with dyslexia. You can now find Olivia's app, named after her, at: http://www.oliviareader.com. Olivia has since been awarded the title of Young Person's Ambassador for the BDA. Let her voice be heard!

With the kind permission of the Loder family, here is Olivia's original handwritten letter, followed by a version typed by her dad, Tim, which was sent with Olivia's letter. Michael Gove did respond to her letter and thanked her for taking the time to write. It's clear that Olivia is passionate about helping other young people with dyslexia and I want to thank her for sharing her journey with us.

Dear Micheal Gove

I'm a dyslexic 11 year old. I am eventually
going to moon hall college a dyslexic school.
I've been to 3 sats schools, my first one was
when I was 4 to 5 I was very badly bullied
and got now help at all and that lead to
getting alepecia. My second school was
when i moved house I went to another
school state, I was there from the age of 6 to 8
It was horrible I got no help either and
was bullied to, I hated school so much
I was skyveing so much. Since we got
my ed sye report already, I went to
moon hall school It was the best Thing
that ever happend I was there from the
age 8 to 11 & my reading age went from age 6
(roughly) to age 16 soit a shows what dyslex
That of course I left year six to go to
high school me and my parents thought I
could handle state again, but we wear
Wrong! I went there for 3 weeks and it
was horrible. So my mums who id a
specilist dyslexic T.A. And being an amazi
parent decided to home school me. It was
good but not the best and we knew
about moon hall So we got a place and
hear I am! The reason I'm writing is
to tell about how state schools
treat dyslexics and feel we feel like
we have no potention and feel like the
thing you found on this the beam of

your shoe and thats not nice.
So thats why children like me should
be getting more help or a temporary
dyslexic School or some help at least
because every one has been through and
you just give a big big big Big
sighing relege. The 4 yes only

4 dyslexic schools in the country are
very expensive my mum started work
there to to help pay the fees. There
should be more help so I olivia toder a
not very much diffent then an other kid
but wanting to make a a big diffent
with the kids like me we can get a good
education and i also will end up teaching
how acting and knowing that to make
a diffent in education.

So mr Michael Grove to take
people like me in to serious consderation

Thank you   My adre
Olivia Toder
11 6/12/13

Dear Michael Gove

I'm a dyslexic 11 year old. I am fortunately going to Moon Hall College, a dyslexic school. I've been to 3 state schools, my first one was when I was 4 to 5. I was very badly bullied and got no help at all and that lead to me getting alopecia.

My second school was when I moved house. And I went to another state school. I was there from the age of 5 to 8. It was horrible. I got no help either and was bullied too. I hated school so much I was skiving so much (feigning illness). Since we got my Ed syc report already I went to Moon Hall School. It was the best thing that ever happened. I was there from the age of 8 to 11. My reading age went from age 6 (roughly) to age 16 so it shows that difference.

Then of course I left year six to go to high school. Me and my parents thought I could handle state again, but we were WRONG! I went there for 3 weeks and it was horrible so my Mum who is a specialist dyslexic TA and being an amazing parent decided to home school me. It was good but not the best and we knew about Moon Hall so we got a place and here I am!

The reason I'm writing is to tell about how state schools treat dyslexics and that we feel like we have no potential and feel like that thing you found on the bottom of your shoe and that's not nice.

So that's why children like me should be getting more help or a temporary dyslexic school or some help at least because everyone has been through and you just give a big, big, big BIG sigh of relief.

The 4 yes only 4 dyslexic schools in the country are very expensive. My Mum started working there (Moon Hall College) to help pay the fees. There should be more help so I, Olivia Loder, a not very much different than another kid but wanting to make a big difference with kids like me can get a good education and I also will end up acting and knowing that I'm making a difference in education.

So Mr Michael Gove take people like me in to serious consideration.

Thank you

Olivia Loder

6/12/2013

The other Olivia is Ian Gilbert's 20-year-old daughter who is also dyslexic. Although schoolwork has always been a struggle for her, she has not only passed her International Baccalaureate (IB) diploma but is now at the Royal Welsh College of Music and Drama studying jazz (remember how important it is to help dyslexic children to find their gift!). In a conversation with her dad, she remarked that she actually enjoyed being dyslexic. When asked why, she came up with the **RESOURCE** on page 46.

10 things I love about being dyslexic

by Olivia Gilbert

Theirs more to life.

1.

As a mature dyslexic, you've learned that asking for help isn't a bad thing.

2.

Dyslexia pushes you to find other ways of expressing the talents you do have.

3.

People are more forgiving if you spell something, reasonably simple, wrong.

You are **here.**

YOU CAN DO IT!

4.

You learn the true value of 'personal best'.

5.

You learn your weakneses.

6.

You become far more eager to push yourself because it doesn't come easy.

CHUFFED TO BE ME

7.

Your schoolwork is always more colourful.

8.

You'll find that you think very differently to the people around you.

9.

You learn the lesson that desiring to try to be better than other people is a waste of time.

WORLD, BRING IT ON!

10.

Once you've learned that not being able to read doesn't make you stupid, you're pretty much **indestructible!**

6

MARMITE GROUP WORK – LOVE IT OR LOATHE IT!

Q I WANT MY CHILDREN TO WORK IN GROUPS, BUT MY HEAD OF DEPARTMENT INSISTS THAT CHILDREN SIT IN ROWS. I HAVE HEARD SOME POLITICIANS INSIST THAT GROUP WORK DOESN'T WORK. WHAT SHOULD I DO?

A I like your style! You do not need your head of department's permission to address the learning needs of your children. If you have seen how group work sparks creative thinking, dialogue and debate and turns a classroom into an adventure playground of children sharing their thinking and ideas, then go ahead!

I find children sitting in rows too regimental. Some would argue that this is a good thing, but it often means that much of the teaching is didactic and does not offer a wide and varied learning experience for the children. If you then want them to work in groups it takes ages just to move the chairs and tables. (And that's if you have tables: some schools don't even have that. I'm thinking about my recent trip to Ghana where the children were squashed onto small wooden benches. When I asked them to move the benches to the side of the room and to sit where they wanted, they naturally congregated in communities of learning – groups! The lessons immediately had a much better feel to them.)

Children who work in groups or teams develop better listening skills, they learn how to share, how to compromise and how to spark ideas from each other. Collaboration between peers means that one child sharing an idea might trigger a different thinking process in another, which hooks into something which yet another has suggested, or it might even give energy to an idea which has not even been thought of yet.

An interesting study into group work by the Institute of Education at University College London (UCL) looked at over 4,000 pupils aged between 5 and 14.[1] It made recommendations that teachers should think of themselves as coaches, but I like to think of them as 'learning mentors' – guiding groups rather than instructing them. When a teacher guides a group of learners, rather than directing them, they are able to solve problems differently. It allows the freedom of individual and group thinking to come together harmoniously. Also, when you have different personalities in a group, you are more likely to get varied and interesting responses and each learner can feel valued for their thinking. The study also found that working in groups enabled children to have their own voice within that group, and so made them more confident in sharing their individuality. They then made better and more rapid progress, and their behaviour also improved.

In some areas of the curriculum group work is an essential part of learning. Take PE – you can never learn about or play football unless you are in a team, and everyone has their role and importance within that team. The same goes for music groups, bands, choirs and so on. I think other subject areas choosing *not* to work in groups could be seen as a form of stifling thinking and reducing young people's ability to learn from each other. It's just like pressing the mute or pause button: only answer when asked to respond! In my view, it's an unhealthy way of learning.

Some teachers involved in the UCL study reported that they found it hard not to intervene in the research project. One teacher said: 'At first we watched and supported groups of children as they argued, shouted, sulked, cried or even stormed off. We were very tempted to intervene, but the researchers said it was important that the children worked through these difficulties.' This is a learning opportunity in itself and allows children to understand that everyone's thinking is as important as their own.

If you still need to convince your head of department that group work is a good idea then you may want to share the following thinking with them (not that you need to because, as the classroom leader, you are there to get the children to experience the best learning progress they can and you will do that in whatever way you see fit).

---

1 See Peter Blatchford, Ed Baines, Christine Rubie-Davies, Paul Bassett and Anne Chowne, The Effect of a New Approach to Group-Work on Pupil–Pupil and Teacher–Pupil Interaction, *Journal of Educational Psychology* 98 (2006): 750–765.

THINK about:

● Group work makes learning more interactive, efficient and fun.

● When working with others, children can pool ideas, listen, see and experience problems or individual thinking from a totally different perspective – I like to call it 'new wave thinking'.

● Group work allows individuals to attempt tasks they could not accomplish on their own, developing a variety of skills and expertise in preparation for tackling more complex challenges at a later date.

● When working together on a timed task, groups can analyse topics in greater depth and breadth than if they are a lonesome thinker or problem-solver.

● Children learn from each other in groups – not just academic learning but interaction, empathy and teamwork.

● Feedback, questioning and presenting a group's work is a skill in itself, and children need to decide among themselves what are the crucial parts to share.

● Group work develops generic skills such as organisation, delegation, effective verbal and physical communication, cooperation, leadership, following and consolidation. These are valuable skills to be used in their learning path through school.

● Group work through play means that children get to experience sharing, caring and discovery. It's that special thing we call 'curiosity, awe and wonder'. Whenever a child has one of those 'Woohoo!' moments in learning it tends to stick, like Super Glue. It's just amazing. That's why we should never stop playing as adults!

● When working in groups, children can share their personalities as well as their thinking.

You may also want to **TRY** the following and share your findings with your head of department:

● Video groups of children working together so that she can see the power of their thinking and collaboration. This is also evidence of oracy, problem-solving and strategic thinking in action.

- When the group presents their work, give them a space where they can show off their hard work. This could be a virtual space, wall space or even an assembly. Showing and sharing can be one of the most powerful tools to recognise and celebrate learner progress.

- Collect some research studies about the power of group work. There are hundreds to be found on the web and in education journals. Share them in your next meeting. Group work is nothing new, but as I mentioned earlier, some teachers see it as Marmite – love it or loathe it!

- Invite your head of department into a lesson and share the thrill of seeing and hearing children working together. It's the power of the children's learning that will sway their thinking – well, you'd hope so anyway!

- A good, forward-thinking head of department will embrace any idea or practice that shows children are engaged and learning. If not, then maybe your departmental head needs to evaluate her own pedagogical thinking!

- When it comes to politicians passing opinions on education, what do they know? What's more, politicians collect in large groups to discuss ideas and thrash out their thinking, so why wouldn't they want children to do the same? It just means that the people who have 'advised' them about policies and practices are a little too narrow-minded when it comes to learning for *all* children.

In a nutshell, every teacher uses various tools for teaching and learning, and group work should definitely be one of those tools. And while we're on the subject of what every teacher can do ...

- Every teacher should know their children well enough to understand what sparks their interests and go to work with a burning desire to question, motivate and engage each child.

- Every teacher should give children wide and varied opportunities to discover learning in different ways – it's that learning buffet again (see Chapter 2).

- Every teacher should want the best for each child, regardless of their learning and living differences.

- Every teacher should embrace new ideas for developing thought-provoking lessons which have rigour, diversity and a plethora of exciting learning opportunities.

- Every teacher should be willing to watch, learn and share ideas in a collaborative learning network.
- Every teacher is a leader in their classrooms – and leaders lead by example.

There's a **RESOURCE** for you on page 52.

A colleague of mine and superb blogger, Rachel Jones (@rlj1981), is a wonderful teacher and inspired a group of 'turned off' sixth-form students through effective group work. You might want to check out her blog post called 'My Best Ever Lesson': http://createinnovateexplore.com/my-best-ever-lesson/. It is part tribute to Robin Williams, part celebration of group dynamics and people coming together to make a difference. Take a look – maybe you could share it with your head of department too.

COMING TOGETHER: *Beginning*

KEEPING TOGETHER: *Progress*

WORKING TOGETHER: *Success!*

MAKE YOUR GROUP *Fizz!*

Resource from *Of Teaching, Learning and Sherbet Lemons* © Nina Jackson, Paul Wrangles, 2015

7

THEY WILL IGNORE YOU UNTIL THEY NEED YOU

Q I HAVE PUPILS IN MY CLASS WHO WILL NOT STOP TALKING – THEY JUST CHAT ALL THE TIME AND THEY AREN'T MAKING PROGRESS. IF THEY AREN'T TALKING TO EACH OTHER THEN THEY ARE TALKING TO PEOPLE ACROSS THE ROOM, AND NOW OTHERS ARE STARTING TO JOIN IN TOO. I'M GETTING NERVOUS ABOUT MY LESSONS AS THEY SEEM TO BE IGNORING ME. CAN YOU HELP?

A It's good to see that you are concerned about the constant chit-chat and that you have the pupils at the heart of your concerns. Well done for asking a very honest and difficult question, as many teachers would be afraid to confess that this is a problem. Fear not, we can work this out and get you and your pupils working and talking together about what counts – learning, thinking and understanding your role and needs as a teacher, as well as their own roles and needs. It's about developing learning and thinking relationships so that you can talk about learning rather than the pupils simply ignoring you.

First, let's take a step back. I want you to ask yourself, when are they talking? Are they talking during your teacher instructions – when you are giving directions or tasks? Or are they talking when you have set the tasks and learning work? There is a big difference between these two scenarios. There can be non-essential chit-chat between friends, but there can also be constructive, creative talk *if* it's happening during a task.

One of the worst things we can do as teachers is to stop pupils from talking to each other about their learning, about what they are discovering or thinking. This is very different to social chatter. If pupils are still discussing an idea or something based on a task or question you have set, and if they are engaged in effective, thought-provoking dialogue, then be the coach and use the tactic of saying, 'Hold those thoughts for a moment, and I will let you continue when we have consolidated our thinking as a class or group.'

Some children are very good at carrying out assignments and being 'on task' while talking about something completely random. This is a strength in itself – they are keen and effective multi-taskers! Use learning talk as a tool to assess progress, but when it's just chit-chat then use either a verbal cue, a facial expression (like 'the look' – every teacher should have 'the look'!) or some teachers even advocate clicking their fingers in the direction of the chatterboxes while continuing to address the rest of the class. These non-verbal signs can be very powerful and show that you are in control, without it interrupting you mid-flow and affecting your teaching with all the pupils.

Spend some time thinking about three non-verbal cues you could use to show you want the pupils to stop talking and listen to you or each other, and three verbal cues to get them to focus on a particular task. The 'power of three' is a good tool as pupils are more likely to remember it and so get used to such habits of learning. The brain seems to remember groups of three much better than any other number.

You may also want to think about working together *with* the pupils to create an appropriate behaviour for learning system in your class. Make sure you work with them to create these acceptable behaviours so that they own them, not you. You can then make reference to this when an individual has chosen not to be part of the class behaviour for learning system – it is more powerful because they have created it themselves. This is very different from you dictating or directing everything they need to do or say.[1]

Just remember that as human beings we are inherently social creatures and we tend to do a better job when we talk to each other. So, if they are a naturally chatty group, then we need to look for teaching and learning strategies that involve lots of dialogue. If, however, they are talking because they are disinterested in the task or activity, or bored with the content of the lesson, then we need to tackle that differently.

---

1   Ian Gilbert supports this view in chapter 2 of his book, *Essential Motivation in the Classroom*, 2nd edn (Abingdon: Routledge, 2012). And I have to say, I'm with him all the way.

So, be honest with yourself. Do you have the confidence and courage to ask them why they talk so much? You might not always like what you hear, but this will be your foundation for the development of great things in future lessons. The pupils will love the fact that you are showing an interest in what they think and want – and that is to be celebrated. We've all had natterers and chatterers, but it's what we do with them that counts.

THINK about when you were in school. I'm sure there were times when you would have preferred to gossip with your friends and classmates rather than listen to the teacher. Ask yourself why you did it, and why you didn't want to, or choose to, listen to the teacher. This will also help you introduce a more human element into your thinking for learning and future planning.

TRY some of these strategies alongside developing some your own:

- Introduce the idea of 'me time–you time–our time'. This is when you have time to talk and the students listen; they have time to talk to each other; and then, as a class, you have time to talk and listen to each other. It's also a very good assessment for learning technique. Make sure you use the verbal cues you have devised for this technique – practise these enough times with the class and you can shorten the cues to just saying 'Me', 'You' or 'Our'. It's a winner. I have observed lots of teachers use this technique and seen how it has resolved many of their concerns. Give it a go!

- Another idea is 'think time–share time' (or 'play time–work time'). While individual think time might occur alone quietly, or even silently, it can also be done in other ways. You can write your thinking, doodle your thinking, speak your thinking, record your thinking or even store your thinking. Share time can take place in many different ways too. Your learners can choose an area in the class where they can display their thinking and learning or note it in a learning log or maybe even on a class/individual blog. Remember that thinking can also be shared or banked. My pupils loved 'bank thinking' (saving it for another time) and 'pigeon thinking' (where they would flock around the room sharing their thoughts with other pupils – and me, of course).

- Make sure you are constantly monitoring and redirecting talk when it's adversely affecting the learners' progress. Move around the room or the learning space observing the situation – when they know you are fast approaching they will get back to the job in hand. Be their guider and mentor, coach and supporter, as well as their director and monitor. You might like to use a key prompt like, 'So, tell me, what have you been discussing so far?' which means you haven't singled them out in front of the others. They will respect you for that — it's another total winner.

● Try a 'talk and share' wall, 'graffiti chat' or something similar, which will allow the pupils to write up their learning talk in a space where others can see it. This can then become a prompt for future discussions. It gives pupils independence and a space to own their thinking talk, and they can complete it at any point during, before or after the lesson. This is yet another great assessment for learning tool which I used to love, because I could graffiti my own learning thoughts about the lesson too!

● At the end of the lesson, try introducing a 'talk token' for any pupil to write their thinking on, or ask them for a written question and put it in a large glass jar when they leave the lesson. Some teachers like to call this strategy 'exit tokens' or 'learning tags'. Watch the jar fill, and then collate evidence of their learning or further questions they might have for you or the class.

Don't forget to evaluate your own teacher talk too. Great teachers can talk, but brilliant teachers choose to talk less and coach more! It's all about pupil progress, not about teachers standing at the front holding forth for the whole lesson.

Finally, please don't worry if you have a chatty class. We've all had them. In my opinion, a chatty class is better than a silent class. Now that is scary! If the pupils are chatting and rudely ignoring you, then think about your school discipline or behaviour policy. If they are stopping others from learning, or it's affecting their own progress, then you need to warn them (quietly and privately at first) that this is not acceptable and that if they choose to continue having a detrimental effect on the learning then you will have no choice but to abide by the terms of the school behaviour system. More often than not, a calm, polite, non-threatening warning is enough. But if it isn't, then make a professional judgement about what you need to do. You know your school system for discipline and behaviour, so use it consistently and fairly, and there will always be mutual respect.

 Here's a **RESOURCE** you might like to use.

Resource from *Of Teaching, Learning and Sherbet Lemons* © Nina Jackson, Paul Wrangles, 2015

8

PUSHY PARENTS

Q I HAVE A PARENT WHO IS VERY FORCEFUL AND BOSSY WHEN SHE DEALS WITH ME. I KNOW SHE WANTS WHAT'S BEST FOR HER SON, BUT I HAVE 29 OTHER CHILDREN TO THINK ABOUT TOO. DO YOU HAVE ANY TIPS FOR DEALING WITH PUSHY PARENTS?

A Your question raises a number of important points, so I'm going to unravel some of the key issues you've mentioned first:

- You say you're being faced with a 'forceful and bossy' parent, but in what sense? Is it to do with the demands being placed on you as a teacher meeting their son's learning needs, or are they telling you that he should be getting better grades?

- If you have 29 other children in the class, then do you view them all as one homogenous group of learners?

- I can give you tips for dealing with pushy parents, but you might also want to consider your own approach to each individual child. Are you, in fact, anxious about meeting the learning needs of all your pupils such that they are making progress in learning and life?

Professor Tanya Byron has observed that pushy parents are increasingly 'stressing pupils' and many youngsters are so frightened of getting bad grades that they are suffering from stress and never develop the 'emotional resilience' needed to succeed in later life.[1] It's true that many of our young people are in fear of upsetting their

---

1 Quoted in Alasdair Glennie, Pushy Parents 'Stressing Pupils': Expert Says Growing Number of Children Are Risking Their Mental Health Because They Are So Terrified of Getting Bad Results, *Daily Mail* (22 May 2014). Available at: http://www.dailymail.co.uk/news/article-2635736/Pushy-parents-stressing-pupils-Expert-says-growing-number-pupils-risking-mental-health-pressure-deliver-grades.html/.

parents or letting them down by not getting the grades they hope they can achieve, which can lead to them being so anxious that their academic progress slows down rather than accelerates.

Some would argue that this is just parents wanting the best for their children, but there is a dramatic difference between pressure and unconditional positive support. Pupils are already under enough pressure from teachers to meet their predicted targets according to summative assessment data, so additional hassle from parents to achieve first-class exam results isn't always in the child's best interest, particularly if it's about doing better than 'the Jones's' and boasting about their talented offspring at the local golf club!

So, I have one further question: do unhappy pupils with top grades make great lifelong learners? I suggest probably not. Some students regard not getting top grades as a personal failure. As a result, they don't benefit from a deep learning experience as they are constantly revising or, worrying about failure or not meeting the expectations of their parents or teachers. In the most serious cases this can lead to self-harm.

It's a different matter if the pupils themselves strive to be the best they can be, because their 'best' might mean getting a G grade – for some that is the equivalent of an A*, depending on their learning and living differences.

Parents should be, and most are, very proud of their children, regardless of their academic achievements, and celebrate their individual gifts and talents. Moreover, most parents love their children – it's simply the consequence of having a child. It's the communities and social circles around families that often dictate whether parents are positively supporting their children, or positively pushing them beyond their capabilities.

The Good Schools Guide has noted that some parents are going to extreme lengths to ensure their children impress admissions teams, with parents of children as young as 3 drilling them in interview techniques to help them get into the country's 'top' prep schools.[2] A wonderful piece of origami would impress me, not a plethora of long-winded intellectual words dropped into a sentence!

So, how can you deal with pushy parents?

---

2 Graeme Paton, Three-Year-Olds 'Coached to Get Into Top Private Schools', *Daily Telegraph* (11 February 2013). Available at: http://www.telegraph.co.uk/education/educationnews/9860555/Three-year-olds-coached-to-get-into-top-private-schools.html/. Shameful, just shameful.

THINK about these strategies and then **TRY** them out during your next meeting with the parent:

- Focus on *all* of the child's achievements – academic, social, emotional and developmental.

- Explain that the personal and emotional development of their child is as important as grades and test scores. The more things you can highlight that the child has done well, the more the parent can celebrate them (and shout at the top of their voices at the golf club!).

- Share some examples of their child's work, such as photographs of them working in groups, discussing problems with others or just happily playing with a big beaming smile on their face. Also include examples of extra-curricular activities, as well as academic tasks, so that you keep focusing on the whole child.

As for the other 29 pupils in the class, as an experienced teacher you will no doubt be meeting the needs of all learners if you are giving them wide and varied learning experiences, in which case they will be making academic and personal progress on a daily basis. Your assessment procedures will highlight where you need to support the most vulnerable learners as well as the gifted and talented ones (and the ones with pushy parents!). And, most importantly, never forget the middle-of-the-road pupils who just seem to coast along very nicely. It's often the 'coasters' who need more of your attention through personal coaching and mentoring.

So, you see, what you are doing is celebrating each individual child for who and what they are. Why don't you become a 'pushy teacher' by praising the celebratory moments of a child's learning in front of their parents? You might also like to highlight that passing exams with flying colours does not always a great human being make.

On page 62 is a useful **RESOURCE** for your classroom.

WARNING!

TO US, YOUR CHILD IS MORE THAN A NUMBER

TEST SCORES ARE IMPORTANT, BUT THEY'RE NOT THE WHOLE PICTURE!

WE TEACH THE BIG PICTURE...

CREATIVITY, EMPATHY,

INTEGRITY, INDEPENDENCE, COMPASSION,

RESPONSIBILITY, COURTESY, DEMOCRACY, LOYALTY, TOLERANCE,

TRUSTWORTHINESS, CITIZENSHIP, SELF-RESPECT, PUNCTUALITY, RESPECT, FAIRNESS,

THOUGHTFULNESS, RESILIENCE, PERSEVERANCE, UNDERSTANDING, DEPENDABILITY, DILIGENCE

Resource from *Of Teaching, Learning and Sherbet Lemons* © Nina Jackson, Paul Wrangles, 20

9

GETTING THE HUGGERS TO BEHAVE

Q A FEMALE CHILD KEEPS COMING TO ME FOR A HUG AND, AS A MALE PRIMARY SCHOOL TEACHER, I FEEL VERY UNCOMFORTABLE ABOUT THIS. WHAT SHOULD I DO?

A First things first, contrary to popular belief, there is no law prohibiting teachers from hugging children. As a male teacher you need to trust your professional judgement on when it is appropriate to hug a child. For example, it would be appropriate if the child was hurt or distressed and had initiated the hug. At such times, it is part of the teacher's role to comfort, reassure and protect the child. It would be inappropriate for a teacher to randomly hug a student for no reason. My own approach is to respond to a hug (i.e. hug back instead of freezing in terror) if a child initiates one.

 I suggest you **THINK** about these questions:

- Are you uncomfortable because you think you will get into trouble?
- Are you uncomfortable because you are not sure what the school policy is?
- Are you uncomfortable because the child is female?

If your answer to any of these questions is yes, then I would strongly recommend that you speak to your head teacher about the school policy on hugging, and also to the child's parents to find out if they are happy for you to hug their child, subject to the caveats above (if need be, get it in writing to cover yourself).

Hugging is a normal part of human behaviour. When we see someone who needs to be comforted, it is quite natural for most of us to want to console them physically. We all need a cuddle from time to time, that's just how it is. Hugs are one of the most beautiful things that can happen to a person (we Welsh have our own word for them – it's called a *cwtch*, and a *cwtch* is a very special sort of hug). When you are hugged you feel good and safe. A proper hug isn't simply a display of affection but a genuine act of caring. Cuddles are one of the best ways to define friendships and loving adult relationships (although here I am referring to the hugs that children need to feel reassured, comforted and safe).

There are proven benefits to hugging too – to the hugger and the huggee. For example, hugs boost our immune system, they can help to alleviate aspects of depression, reduce stress and induce sleep. They are invigorating, rejuvenating and need no batteries. Hugs also replenish our own emotional batteries and have no unpleasant side effects. In fact, a hug is wholesome, organic, naturally sweet and contains no pesticides, no preservatives and no artificial ingredients, and is totally fat free (even a *cwtch*)!

A famous quote by psychotherapist Virginia Satir goes: 'We need four hugs a day for survival. We need eight hugs a day for maintenance. We need twelve hugs a day for growth.' Now, that's a lot of hugging! I can't be sure whether those exact numbers have been scientifically proven, but there is a great deal of research evidence related to the importance of hugs and physical contact, and why, as we grow from babies until the day we leave this earth, hugging is a crucial part of living, learning and well-being.

 THINK about these aspects of hugging.

HUGGING IS A STIMULANT

When we physically hug someone, the hormone oxytocin is released into the body. Oxytocin is a neurotransmitter that acts on the limbic system, which is at the emotional centre of the brain and makes us feel good. Research from the University of California suggests that it has a civilising effect on human males, making them feel more connected with their own emotions and those of others. It is also a social bonding mechanism in relationships. You should also be aware that oxytocin lowers the heart rate and the levels of cortisol in our bodies. This can help to decrease the threat of heart disease.

HUGGING FOR TOLERANCE AND PATIENCE

When we take time to think and understand others we make connections. Hugging is a great way of showing another person that you care and are aware of their personal needs – a hug can take away all the stresses and strains of daily life. Physical interaction with others also makes us feel emotionally well. Simple really: emotional well-being stimulates cognitive development and understanding.

HUGGING AS COMMUNICATION

Sometimes when we make connections with others, words do not form part of the connection chain but hugging does. It's the best way of expressing yourself in a physical way. When we hug each other, it can help us to feel safe and confident in our ability to take on challenges and make complex decisions. It's a reassurance tool as well as an emotional one.

HUGGING AS A CONFIDENCE BOOSTER

Touch is important to us all, but especially with new-born babies and infants. A baby can recognise its parents from their aroma and from the special way they touch and hold them. This is one of the first things babies experience when they are born, and hugging and holding help to create that bond. The cuddles we received from our parents (hopefully) while growing up remain imprinted at a cellular level, so hugs remind us of that love at a somatic level. Hugs, therefore, connect us to a time when we were loved unconditionally and, in turn, help us to self-love. When children don't experience this they can develop reactive attachment disorder in later life. As children in schools don't have their parents close by, they need the reassurance that they are loved unconditionally which a hug from a teacher can provide.

Do you feel better about hugging your pupils now?

It is a sad reflection of today's society that some people instantly jump to the wrong conclusion when they hear about teachers hugging children. All of the teachers I know care deeply about the general health and well-being of their pupils, as well as their education. We see them for an average of seven hours a day, often more than their parents do, so it's hardly surprising that they sometimes turn to us for a comforting or reassuring cuddle. We would be lacking in our duty of care if we just brushed them aside and ignored them.

TRY these strategies to help out with your situation:

- Find out the school policy on hugging (remember, 'touching' is different).
- Speak to the child's parents.
- Ask other teachers about their experiences.
- Speak to the children in your school about hugging and ask them what a hug means to them.
- Ask yourself again what you are most concerned about with regards to hugging.

There's a little **RESOURCE** for you on page 67.

Hug me teacher, keep me safe ~ Hug me so that my learning takes place ~ Hug me just to show you care ~ Thank you teacher — hugs take away my learning scare!

Resource from *Of Teaching, Learning and Sherbet Lemons* © Nina Jackson, Paul Wrangles, 2015

10

SPECIAL LEARNING SPACES

Q I LET SOME OF MY CHILDREN SIT UNDER THE TABLE TO WORK WHEN THEY WANT TO, BUT THE HEAD SAW THIS ONE DAY AND TOLD ME OFF. BUT THEY ARE LEARNING WELL! WHAT SHOULD I DO?

A Under the table learning – how exciting (I just hope there were no sticky bits of chewing gum on the floor!). Special places can have magical qualities that inspire young people to work well. Every person is different, individual and unique, so I am thrilled to hear that you give your pupils opportunities to work in places where they learn well. Well done you!

For many children, special learning places can make them feel both safe and energised. If President Obama called a meeting in an underground cave, instead of the usual Whitehouse Cabinet Room, would that be acceptable? If Richard Branson held a brain-storming meeting at Legoland, would that be acceptable? It would be if the environment proved itself to be stimulating and the quality of ideas that came out of the meeting were different from what they would have been otherwise.

Some children need to be under the table because sitting in front of, behind or even on the table is too ordinary and their thinking demands an extraordinary place to work. If your children learn well when they are under the table, then it has obviously become their special learning den.

Special learning places are unique to us all. But when we are children, finding one that keeps us safe and often hidden away from adults can be the most exciting and mysterious world for play and learning. For me, I can't think of anywhere better than being underneath a table, especially if I had a comfy cushion and a soft blanket, where

I would feel warm and content. For children, feeling this emotional safety means they then have the confidence to do whatever they want or need to do. Even some challenging tasks can seem less troublesome when in a special learning space.

Being safe in a concealed space can offer a total sense of security – much like having a close hug or cuddle from a parent. Many adults also feel secure and work better if they are in a space which either has a special meaning for them or is far enough away from others that they can't be interrupted, and everything is cosy and warm. Many of our great authors and poets have worked in small and unusual places – think of Dylan Thomas's little writing shed in Laugharne, which was his special learning and writing place (many people get it confused with the Boathouse which was his home). A little tiny shed with beautiful views over four merging estuaries. Now that's a special learning space!

For children, special learning spaces need to have easy access and quick exit routes in case of intruders – teachers or parents! (When discovery, curiosity, awe and wonder happens in a special learning place, who are we to interfere with these magical experiences?) Easy ways in and out also help to stop anxiety in children, while still offering them a safe place to work, hide or play.

Special places come in all different shapes and sizes. It could be a blanket over two chairs, a den or tent under a table, a space under the stairs or even a little shed in the school grounds, such as at Sully Primary School in Penarth where they have a literacy shed. This is like a miniature house but equipped with pens, pencils, paints, books and all things magical for children – oh yes, and for the teachers too!

For your pupils, the benefit of a special learning place is that it can make the learning a magical experience. And when you're a child, magic is one of the most important ingredients for happiness and well-being. A special personal space can be an out of this world experience. Tim Gill, former director of the Children's Play Council, observes: 'It is absolutely essential to remember that children need some time and space away from the adult gaze.'[1] He adds that, when children are in their secret places, 'all kinds of imaginative processes come into play. At the same time, they are experiencing their first taste of independence' – even if it is in under the table! Of course, you will be secretly keeping a watchful eye from a distance and monitoring their learning progress.

---

1 Quoted in Catherine O'Dolan, Why Children Love Secret Hiding Places, *Baby and Toddler* (6 August 2010). Available at: http://www.juniormagazine.co.uk/baby-and-toddler/why-children-love-secret-hiding-places/2473.html/.

If you are concerned about the telling off you've received for allowing your pupils to experiment with where they learn, then you might want to consider a course of supportive action to help justify to the head teacher why these children were under tables. If not, then just continue meeting the diverse needs of your learners. When you mark their work, you might want to add a note about their special learning place – much like geotagging your photos or Tweets!

With this is mind, you might like to **THINK** about the following questions and **TRY** some of these suggestions:

- Is allowing children to learn in different spaces a good or a bad thing? What is it specifically that the head is averse to?

- Knowing that these children do learn well under the table, can you show the head teacher some work to demonstrate why you choose to let them to work in different places?

- Invite the head teacher into one of your lessons to observe the learning. When the children go to their special learning spaces – whether that is under the table or anywhere else – one of them will probably ask the head teacher to join them (because that's what children do). Being asked into a child's special place is an honour, so surely no head teacher would turn down that opportunity!

- Ask the children to draw their special learning places as a creative task or get them to write about what a special learning place means to them. I don't propose this task for the sake of responding to the head teacher's concerns, but to elicit information about how and why the children find these spaces liberating.

- Being under the table is much like a man's need for a shed! It's just that special 'getting away from it all' private thinking space. That's enough – I'm considering my own shed too!

- Feltonfleet School in Cobham have found that treehouses are inspirational learning spaces for children. You might like to share that fact with your head teacher!

- Brett Dye, head teacher of Parc Eglos School, near Helston, couldn't afford £15,000 for a classroom extension, so he bought a double-decker bus for £3,500. The bottom deck is used to teach design technology and the top is used for home economics. The back of the bus is known as the 'thinking space' – and it's bright yellow!

● There is a school in Rhyl, North Wales – Ysgol Bryn Hedydd – which also has its own learning bus, and the children feel it's a special learning space. Interestingly, this bus is also yellow and has been operational since 2012.

Learning happens everywhere, not just behind a desk – think about all the schools in the world which have nothing but a floor. Learning has no boundaries and it certainly has no walls. Celebrating learners' progress is the most important thing for you and your pupils. If they are happy and healthy while learning, then that's a winning combination.

On page 73 is a **RESOURCE** you may like to use.

Here's a web **RESOURCE** link you might like to have look at: http://blog.timpany.com/unusual-classrooms.html.

QUIET READING PLEASE, CLASS!
If anyone needs me, I'll be in my special place!

WHAT SPECIAL LEARNING SPACES CAN YOU CREATE?

Resource from *Of Teaching, Learning and Sherbet Lemons* © Nina Jackson, Paul Wrangles, 2015

11

ACTION RESEARCH IN EDUCATION – MAKING A DIFFERENCE

Q AS PART OF MY MASTER'S PROGRAMME I NEED TO CARRY OUT SOME ACTION RESEARCH IN MY SCHOOL THAT HAS BENEFITS WHEN IT COMES TO RAISING STANDARDS BUT ALSO ALLOWS ME TO COMPLETE MY MASTER'S. I DON'T KNOW WHERE TO START, AND I'M NERVOUS ABOUT TELLING MY TUTOR THAT THIS IS UNFAMILIAR TERRITORY FOR ME. I HEARD THAT YOU HAD CARRIED OUT RESEARCH AND THAT YOU HAD WON AN AWARD FOR YOUR WORK. PLEASE CAN YOU GUIDE ME WITH THE TYPES OF THINGS I NEED TO DO?

A No problem. Grab a cup of tea, get a comfortable chair, sit back, relax and let's have a professional 'sharing moment'. I too was like you – nervous, unsure, didn't want to look silly or stupid and never quite 'got' the academic aspect of educational research when I first encountered it as part of my MA (Ed.) back in 1991. However, I am now a convert, and I can safely say that action research is a great place to start. In fact, for me it's the new chocolate – and no one loves chocolate more than me!

If you've recently tried something different in your classroom and evaluated its impact, or planned your lesson differently after seeing a tool designed to engage students and enhance their learning, or tried something completely new that you were unsure of and saw its impact, then you are already well on the way to being an action researcher. It's as simple as that – almost.

Action research is a systematic process. It allows you to try out different processes, strategies and ways of working in your classroom, or your school, in order to find out what really does work for you and your students. You can take simple changes to a new level by formalising the process. Effective action research requires careful planning and preparation, acting on that planning and then evaluating its impact. Remember, a strategy must have a measurable outcome if you are going to validate its effect.

Action research means testing a theory to see if it has impact on the subjects (or 'clients' as they are sometimes referred to in academic research). Many teachers carry out informal action research on a daily basis without even knowing they are – it's the process of self-evaluating and collating data to see what works and what doesn't. However, to make action research specific, you will need to come up with a hypothesis, produce sets of questions to test this hypothesis, and then collect quantitative and qualitative data in order to report on your theory. I like to think of it as look, think, act and reflect.

This was the model I used when planning my research:

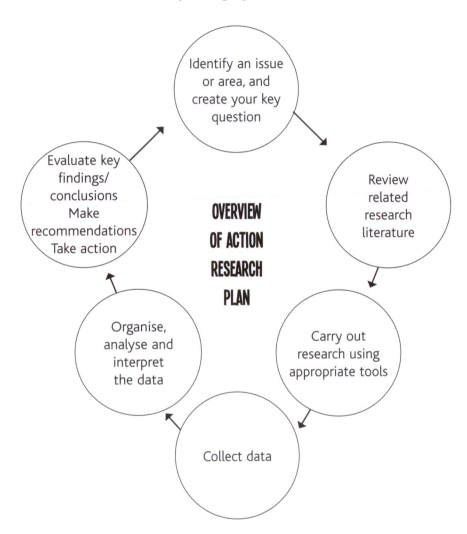

These are the suggested routes you will need to consider, so **THINK** about these processes.

STAGE 1: IDENTIFY AN ISSUE AND BEGIN TO FORMULATE YOUR KEY QUESTION OR HYPOTHESIS

Make the issue relevant to your own teaching and that of others. Don't make it too complicated. Small steps can have a great impact when brought together. An example might be, 'Why do the girls in my class ...?' Then think about how you could develop the question, which might include an intervention such as, 'What happens when ...?'

STAGE 2: FIND OUT MORE ABOUT THE ISSUE OR KEY QUESTION FROM THE RELEVANT LITERATURE. WHAT HAS ALREADY BEEN RESEARCHED AND WRITTEN ABOUT THIS AREA OF STUDY?

Read education articles, research papers, journals and other studies. You might want to look at articles in the *British Educational Research Journal* (BERJ) which is published by the National Foundation for Educational Research (NFER): www.nfer.ac.uk/publications/educational-research/. Your literature research should be an ongoing process, as you will probably want to make adjustments to your research terms as you learn more about your subject.

STAGE 3: CARRY OUT RESEARCH USING APPROPRIATE TOOLS

Before you begin, you will need to collect some baseline data – for example, where are the pupils currently? You may wish to consider what pre-existing statistics you can tap into to find out this information.

You then need to identify a way to measure any progress – for example, you could use testing at the end or collect impact evidence throughout the project. Research tools could include questionnaires, observations, videos, interviews, diaries and so on. This is action research in practice.

The key questions you should be considering are:

1. What am I going to measure?
2. How am I going to measure it?

For my research, I created a teacher pack to help teachers use music in the classroom to raise standards of learning and teaching. The pack included CDs with playlists, questionnaires, learning diaries for the pupils and teaching diaries for the staff. I also conducted interviews and collected evidence using video.

Make sure your research is rigorous and systematic, and keep checking with your colleagues that all is well and they have not forgotten to carry out any of the key tasks. Measuring impact is crucial.

STAGE 4: COLLECT THE DATA

Assemble all the information you have gathered.

STAGE 5: ORGANISE, ANALYSE AND INTERPRET THE DATA

At this point you will need to create a system that allows you to record the data. I set up some simple spreadsheets (and no one hates spreadsheets more than I do!). As you input the data, choose the most appropriate method of presenting and reporting, which could be graphs, comments boxes and so on.

STAGE 6: EVALUATE YOUR KEY FINDINGS, COME TO YOUR CONCLUSIONS AND MAKE RECOMMENDATIONS, THEN TAKE FURTHER ACTION

When you have gathered your data and analysed the results, you will need to ask yourself three key questions:

1.   How would you do things differently?

2.   What have you learned from the research?

3.   What are the main areas of impact, if any?

Reflect on the findings and come to a conclusion about the results. You can then make further recommendations and share these with your colleagues. Hopefully, your hypothesis will have been validated by the qualitative and quantitative data you have gathered, so you will now have firm evidence that it works. Bear in mind that some research does not produce a positive response, but this is all part of the research process. It's about finding out what works and what doesn't, and how it does or doesn't work.

Once you have identified the positive impact of the intervention on learning and teaching, then share, share and share some more – invite your colleagues to a presentation or publish a paper.[1]

 Use the **RESOURCE** on page 81 for inspiration.

 Here are two additional web **RESOURCES** to help with your action research project:

http://study.com/academy/lesson/action-research-in-education-examples-methods-quiz.html

http://www.brown.edu/academics/education-alliance/sites/brown.edu.academics.education-alliance/files/publications/act_research.pdf

It is also worth looking at Louis Cohen, Lawrence Manion and Keith Morrison, *Research Methods in Education*, 7th edn (Abingdon: Routledge, 2011): this excellent book was the foundation of my understanding of research in education.

---

1   My research enabled me to go on and write a book, *The Little Book of Music for the Classroom*.

Resource from *Of Teaching, Learning and Sherbet Lemons* © Nina Jackson, Paul Wrangles, 2015

If you carry out any action research after reading this chapter, do get in touch, won't you? I would love to hear about it.

12

I'VE LOST THAT LOVIN' FEELING

Q I'M AT THE END OF MY TETHER AND I'M THINKING ABOUT LEAVING TEACHING AS IT'S NO LONGER THE JOB I USED TO LOVE. WHAT WITH THE CHANGES IN NATIONAL POLICY, THE INSPECTIONS AND EVERYTHING ELSE, I REALLY FEEL THERE ARE TOO MANY THINGS GETTING IN THE WAY OF ME ACTUALLY DOING WHAT I KNOW MY CHILDREN NEED. WHAT SHOULD I DO?

A How can a question be both sad and happy at the same time? Yours can, and so I thank you for asking it. I'm sorry that you feel you no longer love the job you do. Hopefully, I can help you to see past those things that are getting in the way, and to focus on what is the most important thing in teaching – knowing what your children need from you. I have the sense that you are a passionate and caring teacher who wants only the best for the children you teach. If we could bottle that and pass it on to other teachers, then we would have a truly outstanding profession – one where the heart has been put back into learning.

Are you aware that your sense of justice for the children you teach comes through as your absolute priority? For this reason, I don't believe you have lost your love for teaching, but I can understand how the frustration of all the seemingly peripheral factors which seem to take over our lives as teachers can end up dominating your thinking.

Let's unravel what might really be the issue here and put it all back together so that you find that lovin' feeling once again. I'd like you to **THINK** about the following questions:

- Why did you join the teaching profession?
- What have been the most magical learning experiences for you?
- What have been the most magical learning experiences for your children?
- When was the last time you laughed in class at a pupil's response to something?
- When did you last cry because a child had created something really wonderful or said something beautiful to you?
- Have you tried out any new teaching and learning ideas recently?
- Close your eyes – how many smiling faces can you see from the children you have taught over the years? Capture that moment and make it a picture in your mind.
- When did you last share a teaching and learning idea with a colleague?
- How many times has a child thanked you for being a great teacher (or maybe you can't as there have been so many)?
- If you left teaching, would you miss going shopping for the most hilarious and brilliant pencil case ever?
- Do you see school inspections as a celebration of the great teaching and learning that goes on in your school? If you see it as something else, then try to imagine that it's your special time to show and share the amazing work your children do, and the wonderful impact you have as a teacher.
- Do you always perceive changes in school or educational policies negatively? A change in policy can often mean that a different name is being given to an already established aspect of teaching and learning, so without sounding flippant, you probably just need to think of it as fine-tuning something rather than starting all over again. So, just tweak that paperwork slightly and think about where it fitted in previously.

- What does teaching and learning mean to you? Think about the bigger picture. If it's about doing what we've done forever – that is, giving each child an opportunity to grow up into a healthy 'thinking' adult, able to embrace the world and meet its challenges – then the only thing that has changed over the centuries is the way we do it.

- When was the last time a parent thanked you for helping their child?

- When did you last have a good knees-up with your teaching colleagues and laugh about the 'nonsense' of some policies and practices?

- When was the last time you stopped, thought about *you* and told yourself that you are doing a damn fine job in putting the teaching and learning of the children first. And if you haven't done it recently then stop right there and do it *now*!

 Here are my suggestions for getting that loving feelin' back. **TRY** them and fill your heart with that burning desire you had for teaching before the 'I' word (inspection) and the 'things that get in the way' became such a worry for you. Here we go:

- The most outrageous thing I've ever done in teaching is ... (I can hear you laughing out loud already!)

- The naughtiest thing I've ever done as a teacher is ... (Careful now, you might need an oxygen tank if you're laughing too much!)

- The funniest costume I've ever worn as a teacher is ... (Warning – the real ones, not the fantasy ones, please!)

- My favourite mug for my tea/coffee lives ... (As long as no one takes it without your permission!)

- The best piece of stationery I've ever bought as a teacher is ... (I bet you can't narrow that one down!)

If you could run up and down the school corridors yelling obscenities about the things that get in the way, what 'naughty' words would you shout out and how high would you wave your arms in the total freedom of being able to do so? Go on ... ask the caretaker to let you run free when no one else is there. It will do you the power of good. (Just make sure he turns off the CCTV!) Ooh, I'm visualising it right now and seeing you releasing all that anger as you get that lovin' feeling back!

 There's a **RESOURCE** for you on page 86. Copy it and fill in the boxes, and keep it handy as a constant reminder.

THE THINGS THAT MAKE ME
a Great Teacher!

The things I love about teaching:

The things that make me laugh as a teacher:

My greatest moments in teaching:

My secret list of grumpy teachers who need to start enjoying their job again:

Resource from *Of Teaching, Learning and Sherbet Lemons* © Nina Jackson, Paul Wrangles, 2C

Now add your own list of things that have made you smile over the years and ask yourself, do I really need to let things get in the way of doing what I do best – teach?

At the end of the day, *you* are your own best resource, so if you focus on the reasons why you came into teaching (and you've managed to think about some of those hilarious suggestions above) then I'm confident it will help you to get your lovin' feeling back.

13

STUTTERS AND STAMMERS

Q I HAVE A NEW CHILD IN MY CLASS WHO HAS A STUTTER. I'M NOT SURE IF IT'S A STUTTER OR A STAMMER, AND I'M NOT SURE IF I KNOW THE DIFFERENCE EITHER. DO YOU HAVE ANY TIPS FOR HIM, FOR ME AND FOR HIS CLASSMATES?

A Stuttering is a very unusual living difference – on average one in every 100 people has a stutter or stammer. The severity can depend on how emotionally well the person is feeling at any given time, and each speech difference has its own individual traits. Speech and language difficulties normally occur during early childhood, but they can vary – sometimes it's there and sometimes it's not. This can make it a very frustrating condition for many young people.

Stammering and stuttering is a specialism that even the best scientists and doctors are continuing to grapple with: the exact causes are unknown, although it is thought to be related to the way the brain is wired. Family history also plays a part and it is likely the condition may be inherited. The most important thing you can do for a child who has a speech difference is to allow them to finish sentences, instructions and requests *themselves*. Listen carefully, show a supportive face (your 'Yes, I'm sympathetic to what you're saying' look) but never try to complete what you think they might want to say. This helps no one and, in fact, may damage the child's confidence. An individual with a stutter or stammer knows exactly what they want to say, it's just that they can't get the words out quickly enough.

Many of us get stuck with our words sometimes, and for some reason they don't come out quite right. Some people hear themselves saying what they want to say before they actually say it. Knowing what you want to say, but the words not coming out in the right order, can be a confusing situation for the brain. We then get anxious because we fear we're not making sense. If you don't have a stutter or stammer, then maybe this will give you an insight into how distressing that moment can be. It can make the process of speaking in front of others very stressful, especially in a class setting.

It's probably worth mentioning at this point what the difference is between stuttering and stammering. It's quite simple really. Stuttering is when you say the first bit of a word but can't stop saying it over and over – like this: *St-st-st-stuttering* ... Stammering, on the other hand, is when you get stuck after the first bit of the word – like this: *St* ... *ammer* ... Furthermore, the 'ingredients' of stammering or stuttering will be different for each individual.

 THINK about this: as we would for every child in our classroom, we need to take into account their individual learning and living differences. Developing a healthy, open relationship, which shows you care about their well-being and emotional health, is as important as academic progress and curriculum needs. Ask the child if he can tell you how best to support his stuttering difficulty. You may be very surprised at the effect this will have. By approaching a difficult problem in a relaxed way, you should be able to improve the situation and help him in the classroom and around the school.

 TRY these tips for helping a child who stutters:

- Provide consistent feedback to him about his speech in a friendly, non-judgemental and supportive way. Remember the four-to-one praise ratio I spoke about in Chapter 5. Every little helps!

- Don't react negatively when he stutters. Give any corrections in a gentle way, and give praise when he speaks without a stutter.

- Listen carefully when he speaks, and wait for him to say the intended word. Don't try to complete sentences for him.

- Talk openly about stammering and stuttering (if he wants to talk about it), and highlight that some of the most creative and able people in the world have stutter and stammer living differences. You might want to create a 'special people with special learning and living differences' display to highlight this to other children, so they can see that it's part of a person's personality and make-up, not just an add-on to who or what they are (have a look at the Stuttering Foundation's 'Famous People who Stutter' poster for some inspiration[1]). These people include:

---

1   See http://www.stutteringhelp.org/famous-people-who-stutter.

- ■ Nicole Kidman – Award-winning actress and film producer.

- ■ Emily Blunt – Multi-award-winning actress in film, TV and theatre.

- ■ Bruce Willis – One of the world's highest grossing actors, best known for the *Die Hard* series.

- ■ Marilyn Monroe – A cultural icon and one of the most popular film stars of the 1950s and early 1960s.

- ■ Tiger Woods – One of the most successful golfers in the world.

- ● Provide a relaxed environment that allows many opportunities for him to speak in class with his peers. This includes making time for students to talk to each other, especially when he is excited and has a lot to say to his fellow students.

- ● Help him to be confident so that he can communicate successfully even when he stutters.

- ● Try speaking in a relaxed and slightly slow way when you respond to him in class. This will help him to identify rhythmic sounds and show him that speaking clearly and slowly is a strength.

You might also want to try using music to help him with his stuttering. In my own research on the effects of music on the brain, it's clear that if someone listens to music through headphones and speaks at the same time, the rhythm of the music gets the brain focused on those sounds rather than other people's voices. Someone who stutters is very aware of others around them and they can become increasingly nervous about speaking when they hear other people talking coherently and without a stutter. Knowing that you have a stutter actually makes the process of thinking about what you are going to say, and then saying it aloud, even more difficult. That's why we must never try to complete a word or sentence for someone with a stutter. It's not only rude, but it can cause emotional harm. Their confidence may already be at rock bottom, and knowing that you are aware of the issue can make getting the words out correctly an even greater problem. Be as sympathetic as you can, and wait, wait and wait some more until they have finished speaking.

You may have seen this technique used with a young man in the documentary series *Educating Yorkshire*. Music helped teenager Musharaf Asghar to overcome his stammer and deliver his end of Year 11 speech in front of the whole school. He received a resounding standing ovation. Very emotional, wonderful and a great personal achievement.

Use the **RESOURCE** on page 93 to help other children understand. I hope this child settles in well and, with your support and these strategies, I'm sure a great learning relationship will develop.

stutter, stammer special me!

Why would I want to be ordinary?
Ordinary is just that – plain
I like being extraordinary
Because quite simply, that's what makes me, me

Me is special, not like you
All those ordinary kids in the class
Even though I stutter and stammer a lot
It makes me special it makes me, me

What makes me, me are my special ways
My stutter, stammer and sticking phase
So, let me speak when it's right for me
Do not finish any sentence or word for thee

Let me be me and you be you,
My stutter, stammer in a queue
The words and phrases will come out
Don't make me angry and want to shout

So, stutter, stammer and special me
Together we are extraordinary
Don't mock me, speak for me or think you're kind
Let me speak at my speed, you'll hear my mind

Why would I want to be ordinary?

No thanks!

Resource from *Of Teaching, Learning and Sherbet Lemons* © Nina Jackson, Paul Wrangles, 2015

14

LET OUR VOICES BE HEARD

Q I HAVE BEEN GIVEN THE RESPONSIBILITY OF SETTING UP A SCHOOL COUNCIL. DO YOU THINK IT'S WORTHWHILE AND, IF SO, DO YOU HAVE ANY ADVICE ON THE BEST WAY TO GO ABOUT IT?

A The benefits of setting up a school council are huge. You are involving the whole school and this can be pivotal for the wider community as well as the individuals involved. Pupils will feel valued and it will provide a basis for the active learning of a range of important and essential life skills. These include speaking and listening skills, teamwork, the development of emotional literacy, moral reasoning, self-esteem, confidence, problem-solving and being part of something bigger than the individual.

Professor Bernard Crick, Chair of the Advisory Group on Citizenship has observed, 'School councils and class councils … can be a most excellent training ground in responsibility for future citizens.'[1] Being involved in a pupil or school council will provide a dynamic foundation for learning for many pupils, especially in the area of citizenship. They are more likely to become resilient in the face of negative experiences, and being part of a school council will give them a voice – they will know that their opinions count. This is an extremely valuable motivational tool for every child.

When you begin thinking about creating a school council, the involvement of the whole school is crucial from the outset – you want everyone to 'own' it. Most importantly, the pupils should choose who they want to represent them – not only to speak for them but also in a way that they can relate to.

---

1   See http://www.globalfootprints.org/whyschoolcouncils.

The benefits of creating a school council, whether at primary or secondary phase, include improved relationships between pupils and between pupils and teachers, increased levels of trust, a greater understanding of pupils' experiences and a more pleasant and equitable school atmosphere.

As well as improving communication skills, negotiation, decision-making and teamwork, a school council can help pupils to feel as if they are making their own stamp on the school. Consequently, they will experience an increased sense of ownership of certain strands of their learning. This is especially the case if the council gets involved in activities like interviewing prospective teachers, governors and school leaders.

Some schools have reported higher levels of attainment, a reduction in pupil exclusions, a decrease in incidents of bullying and an increased awareness of the need for, and participation in, citizenship. Of course, no school will ever be completely free of bullying, but allowing pupils to talk and share their experiences openly will bring a difficult subject to the forefront, with benefits all round for emotional and physical well-being.

 THINK about the following issues when starting to put a plan together.

WHAT A SCHOOL COUNCIL NEEDS:

- That all pupils in the school are involved.
- That it is pupil-led.
- That it becomes part of the school's ethos, practice and mission.
- That it deals with the core issues of the school.
- That it makes a difference to the learning and emotional well-being of all.

TO ENABLE THIS TO HAPPEN THERE HAS TO BE:

- Full and active support from the head teacher and the senior leadership team, so make sure you have a meeting to discuss your plan for the school council and your vision before embarking on anything. Get their support in writing too, maybe in the form of a head teacher's 'pledge'.

- Full integration of pupil participation and a joint decision-making process relating to school issues and policies that directly affect them. By this, I mean *all* relevant aspects of school life, including teaching and learning, and not just the physical environment and fundraising events. A cupcake fundraising event on its own does not a school council make!

- A structure that includes a full system of in-class councils, year groups, houses and class captains or executives. Remember, it's not about giving the 'good' kids a chance, it's about giving every child a chance to represent their peers.

- Regular, formalised meetings that are timetabled (including systematic and appropriate ways for feedback from these meetings to be disseminated), plus sub-councils or sub-committees to involve as many pupils as possible.

- A school council link teacher (you!) who monitors form tutors to ensure that the school council's proposals are presented, discussed and shared with all the children. Being involved in the school council should become a key part of the form tutors' job description.

- Good communication with all staff and the rest of the school about what the school council is planning – no teacher wants to hear about major changes in the school from a pupil in their class. Getting the timing right and sharing with all, including parents and governors, is crucial.

You might want to create a school councillor job description (like the one on page 98). This will not only set out guidelines for the type of pupil the council needs and wants, but it will teach the pupils that every job advert includes a list of the roles and responsibilities. This is the beginning of learning for employment, and it's relevant even in primary schools. It should be part of the extended classroom, the enriched learning curriculum, which I believe embodies the essential skills and learning for life.

TRY this out as a possible job description. It was adapted from one created by the Schools Councils for Wales:

SCHOOL COUNCILLOR JOB DESCRIPTION

IT IS ESSENTIAL THAT YOU:

- Have lots of energy and enthusiasm
- Are able to work properly with other people
- Are good at listening
- Can make good decisions
- Accept the opinions of other people
- Are happy to represent the students
- Are good at explaining things

IT IS DESIRABLE THAT YOU:

- Have lots of ideas
- Like solving problems
- Don't mind if some people don't like what you've done
- Are willing to change your mind if it is the best thing for the school

 Use the **RESOURCE** on page 99 to inspire your school council discussions.

 Here's a useful **RESOURCE**: the Welsh Assembly Government's *School Councils Activity Pack for Pupils and Staff*: www.pupilvoicewales.org.uk/uploads/publications/74.pdf. Of all the documents and toolkits I have seen, this is by far one of the best. It is filled with activities, templates, guidelines and more. The only thing it won't do for you is make a cup of tea and offer you a slice of cake!

Good luck to you all with your school councils – let their voices be heard!

Resource from *Of Teaching, Learning and Sherbet Lemons* © Nina Jackson, Paul Wrangles, 2015

15

DON'T SHOUT OUT!

Q I CAN'T STOP CERTAIN CHILDREN FROM SHOUTING OUT THE ANSWERS WHEN I ASK QUESTIONS. WHAT CAN I DO?

A For some pupils, shouting out answers when you ask questions in class is an unstoppable outpouring of excitement and eagerness – they are just bursting to tell you what they know as quickly as possible. It's a little learning volcano waiting to erupt! As human beings we are all the same, and yet we are all different. Some will shout out the answers, some will smile quietly to themselves and remain silent, even though they know the answers, and some will wait to see what others have to say first to check whether what they are thinking is correct.

Much depends on the type of questions – whether they are knowledge response questions or definitive answers to a numerical or academic question. If they are philosophical questions, then some pupils will want to share their views straight away.

The eagerness a child has to blurt out an answer they know is right can sometimes be difficult to handle in the classroom. Shouting out is good for the soul, but managing the excitement of a child sharing what they know can make your life as a teacher very difficult. You may want to let them all call out in one single flourish and then use a helicopter rotation technique to get them to share their responses one after another. At least the initial shout-out lets them share their thinking immediately and releases the tension of their enthusiasm. Alternatively, let them shout it, then show it or share it in a different way. This will help you with your anxiety around the rowdiness of everyone calling out in one single blurt of excitement.

Remember that your gifted and talented students, who are sometimes deemed the disruptive ones (they tend to shout out because they want to share their thinking immediately), could run to a graffiti wall and write their thinking there or jot it in a learning log. It may just help to lower your blood pressure!

According to a study by academics at Durham University, pupils who shout out answers can be nearly nine months ahead in reading and maths when compared with their quieter classmates.[1] Professor Peter Tymms, head of the School of Education at Durham University and lead author of a study on calling out in class, says, 'It's quite useful for a classroom teacher to know that blurting out helps the individual.'

Boys, in particular, love to shout out – it's part of their hunter nature! Just think of ways in which you could consolidate this as a 'shout it then write it', or a 'shout it then record it' exercise. Remember those audio tools I mentioned in Chapter 2? These are great tools for immediate learning and feedback from pupils. Get that audio learning ready every lesson.

 I think you need to ask yourself about questioning in your classroom and what type of responses you want. **THINK** about these questions:

- Do the same pupils shout out all of the time, or are they different depending on the type of questions you pose?
- Is it you who is uncomfortable about the shouting out, or is it other pupils?
- Do you give the class opportunities to respond to your questions in different ways? If so, what are those differences? There are hundreds of ways you can get pupils to respond to your questions.
- When you ask for responses, is this a way of developing their literacy skills?
- Have you ever introduced a 'mute' button remote control method in your class – like a game for responses?
- Who is allowing them to shout out? You or the other pupils?

As a teacher in a busy, noisy department, shouting out or calling out was one of the strategies I actively encouraged to engage the pupils in a task or activity. However, there are also times when this is inappropriate as it takes away from the successful

---

1 See Jeevan Vasagar, Me, Miss! Why Blurting Out the Answers Can Be Good for Pupils, *The Guardian* (2 February 2012). Available at: http://www.theguardian.com/education/2012/feb/02/blurting-out-answers-good-for-pupils/.

thinking processes of others. Remember, you need to lead the learning and make it clear what is acceptable and what is not. Correct answers weren't the most important thing for me during these tasks – it was more about getting them all involved. 'Allowing' them to shout out was a form of venting as well as a group collaboration exercise. The pupils thought it was a knowledge question task, but, in fact, it was a 'getting ready for action' task that would get them pumped up and ready for some exciting learning.

The sheer excitement of one pupil shouting out can encourage others to become engaged, or perhaps the pupil who cannot help himself from saying something can force the group to face a reality which none are prepared to declare openly. It's the psychology behind the learning game which really counts.

 If you are looking for particular strategies to stop children calling out at inappropriate times, then **TRY** these activities.

PASS THE POM-POM

Ask a question, then use an object (e.g. pom-pom, parcel, ball) and throw it to the pupil you want to answer. Not a heavy object, mind you – we don't want a health and safety investigation!

JOT 3 – TOP 10

I mentioned this strategy in Chapter 2, but you can adapt it to include pupils responding with three different answers that they could jot down on a sticky note, whiteboard, iPad – anything so they can visually hold up their answers. You can then take a photo of their responses and use it as evidence of learning. Ask for a minimum of three responses (so that all your pupils feel included) and a maximum of 10 for those super-keen pupils who will want to share as much as they can with you.

SHOUT IT OUT LEARNING WALL

This strategy uses shouting out as a celebratory mode of thinking and sharing. Make it a game where they place their responses around the learning environment – on a learning wall, in a box or jar, on a window – to see each other's thinking.

DIRTy TIME

This technique was devised by Jackie Beere: DIRT stands for Directed Improvement Reflection Time.[2] Give pupils time to think and respond to questions, and then choose the method in which you would like them to respond. It would be absolutely fine to have DIRTy shouting time, writing time or doodling time – whatever method best suits the learning. After all, the more innovative the ways you think of collating pupil responses to questions, the more you will keep them engaged and meet their diverse learning needs. It's all about differentiation and inclusion.

SNOWBALLING

This method encourages the use of negotiation, empathy and reasoning between your pupils. When asking a question, the pupils first have to produce an answer individually. They then share it with a partner and turn their two answers into one agreed response. The pair then joins up with another pair and repeats the process. This way, four answers are synthesised into one. Some would call this think–pair–share, which is a great strategy for formative assessment and group work. You can call it what you like, but mixing groups of pupils and getting them to work together is very effective.

---

2   Jackie Beere, *The Perfect Ofsted Lesson* (Carmarthen: Crown House Publishing, 2011), pp. 29–30.

THREE'S NOT A CROWD

This is a structured means of eliciting information, developing concepts, understanding and processing what is said, as well as responding to your questions and other pupils' thinking. It also promotes self-awareness through the role of the observer. The pupils work in threes, two sat facing each other, one slightly offset and observing how they interact with each other. Each pupil takes on the role of talker, questioner and recorder. The talker explains something, comments on an issue or expresses an opinion based on questions from you, the teacher. The questioner prompts and seeks clarification and the recorder makes notes and gives a report at the end of the conversation. Next time the roles are changed. The pupils can video the responses rather than taking notes if they prefer.

SEND ME YOUR ANSWER

Ask your students to send their answers to you via the different digital devices you have in your classroom or, if you have a policy of BYOD (bring your own device) you could incorporate those too. When using my iPad in the classroom, I like to use Socrative Teacher/Socrative Student, PollDaddy, Nearpod, Poll Everywhere, PingPong SPOT Networking and Quizlet.

The **RESOURCE** on page 106 gives you a list of the strategies for managing or directing children who want to shout out.

If you want some great **RESOURCES**, check out Mark Anderson at www.ictevangelist.com (@ICTEvangelist) where there are some amazing tutorials. He also has an outstanding book, *Perfect ICT Every Lesson* (Carmarthen: Independent Thinking Press, 2013).

NO SHOUT OUT ACTIVITIES
In Action!

1. Pass the pom-pom
2. Jot 3 – Top 10
3. Shout it out learning wall
4. DIRTy time
5. Snowballing
6. Three's not a crowd
7. Send me your answer

Resource from *Of Teaching, Learning and Sherbet Lemons* © Nina Jackson, Paul Wrangles, 201

16

LEARNING STYLES – WHAT LEARNING STYLES?

Q I USED TO THINK LEARNING STYLES WAS USEFUL IN THE CLASSROOM TO HELP ME ADD SOME VARIETY TO MY LESSONS, BUT NOW IT'S ALL OVER TWITTER THAT THEY'RE RUBBISH. WHAT DO YOU THINK?

A In 1999, when I was a full-time teacher in South Wales, all I heard from the senior leadership team was learning styles, learning styles, learning styles – oh yes, and VAK! There was a trend at that time for students to complete questionnaires about their preferred learning styles. Have you ever heard such nonsense (although some did not think so at the time)? Completing the questionnaire in itself made a mockery of the so-called VAK system. If it was that good, then why not get the pupils to respond in a visual, auditory or kinaesthetic way, rather than using a plain, boring questionnaire? But educationalists love a questionnaire, don't they? And then there was a new trend from the United States called VARK (the R being reading). It was just getting out of hand.

There is no evidence to prove that teaching children using individualised learning style systems improves pupil progress or, for that matter, raises levels of attainment. So, we can dismiss the idea of learning styles, can we? While planning lessons that rely on a three (or four)-pronged approach is now considered a cause for concern, the application of learning experiences is most definitely to be celebrated. After all, if we give our pupils interesting, engaging learning experiences then we do not need to consider segmenting them into VAK-related learning strands. When we offer children a range of learning experiences, we move away from didactic teaching – which is a one-chance, one-model learning strategy. Thinking in terms of VAK helped teachers to start thinking about making learning varied and exciting, so while we might trash the theory we should not overlook its good points.

So what useful concepts might be hiding beneath the learning styles ethos?

- Every pupil is different and these differences affect the way in which they learn. Those who have special needs or are gifted and talented (or have living and learning differences, as I like to call them) need different teaching and learning approaches and experiences. Intelligence comes in a variety of levels and forms.

- Children will always have different interests – things that turn them on and turn them off. Flicking the 'turn me on' switch means that they will learn faster and in more depth, often wanting to develop their learning and thinking independently. Offering a variety of classroom turn ons is definitely the secret to success.

- Because our pupils have such diverse backgrounds, we need to consider the needs of the whole child rather than just the way they learn or what we give them to think about.

Definitely **THINK** about this and **TRY** this idea: I have lots of experience of working with young people and I, and many of my colleagues, know that taking children out of their comfort zone is key to stimulating curiosity and a thirst for learning. By 'comfort zone', I'm referring to the various common strategies, tasks and activities with which they are familiar (design a poster, create a PowerPoint, write an essay, read Chapter 3 and answer the questions, etc.). It's why, as a teacher, I have always believed in continuing professional development (CPD) – professionals continually adding to their repertoire of teaching and learning strategies for engaging learners and putting together that all-important learning buffet (see Chapter 2).

When we introduce new and different ways of thinking and doing the same things, the brain becomes curious and asks questions about 'What's going on here?' We do it naturally as human beings. 'Dare to be different' has always been my motto, and it can be yours too. So, I am daring you to be different by living on the edge and giving your learners novel experiences – oh yes, and you too!

On page 109 is a **RESOURCE** you might want to use to remind others (and yourself) that everyone is different!

Dear teacher...

DIFFERENT WAYS OF LEARNING ARE EXCITING!

We are all different and yet we are all the same!

GIVE US AS MANY DIFFERENT LEARNING EXPERIENCES AS YOU CAN

ONE SIZE DOES *not* FIT ALL!

Resource from *Of Teaching, Learning and Sherbet Lemons* © Nina Jackson, Paul Wrangles, 2015

FEED ME!

Q AS AN NQT, I HAVE HEARD TEACHERS TALKING ABOUT THE IMPORTANCE OF FEEDBACK, BOTH WRITTEN AND VERBAL. PLEASE COULD YOU HELP ME TO UNDERSTAND HOW I PUT THIS INTO PRACTICE. DOES IT REALLY HAVE TO BE POSITIVE ALL THE TIME?

A Feedback can take many shapes and forms, but it should always be framed in a positive way. Essentially, it is a two-way conversation between you and the students, whether it is verbal, written or gestural feedback for an individual, group or whole class. You can also use positive feedback in your marking and through other written or verbal comments. Remember, marking does not always have to be written – you can also mark and give your feedback verbally (although you might want to make a note on the pupils' work that you have given them verbal feedback).

The ultimate goal of positive feedback is to provide your students with an 'I can do' growth mindset. And if they are so motivated by your feedback that it turns into an 'I can do anything' attitude and learning philosophy, then so much the better.

The way that we give feedback to our students can have a positive effect on attainment and pupil well-being, as well as other aspects of education. It's also a great motivational tool, helping pupils rise to the challenge of learning. There's nothing better than seeing a smiling face on a Monday morning when you give positive praise or feedback for work, behaviour or attitude – or for simply being at school on time for some of our students.

Sometimes it's hard to give positive feedback if a student has rumbled your cage, but remember that every day and every lesson should be a new beginning. Wipe that slate clean. As Michelle Pfeiffer told her unmanageable, disgruntled, disengaged and non-learning class at the beginning of the film *Dangerous Minds*, 'There are no victims in this classroom' – and there should never be victims in your classroom either.

It's our job as teachers to ensure that we give our best to our students. If you've ever heard Vic Goddard (head teacher of Passmores Academy, Harlow) or Dave Whitaker (executive principal of Springwell Community School, Barnsley) talk, you will have heard them mention 'unconditional positive regard'. I love this. I've added a Ninja twist and call it unconditional positive support (UPS). It's all about developing effective relationships for learning – and not holding grudges about the things they once did to annoy you!

There is a two-strand approach to positive feedback:

1. For the students as learners it is based on assessment for learning (i.e. it's about attainment and achievement within the curriculum and is learner focused).

2. For the teachers it is based on their personal approach, application and presentation (i.e. a more humanistic approach, valuing each and every child for who and what they are).

 Putting positive feedback into practice starts with some considerations and some questions. **THINK** about:

● How well do you know your students?

● How well do you know what they are able to achieve? How do you know this?

● Do you have some SEND children who need additional support?

● Who are the more able/gifted and talented pupils? What are their strengths, and what areas do they need to develop?

● Do you need to change the language you use for different students? (This is known as differentiated feedback and ranges from simple to complex language.)

● How well have your students responded when you have given positive praise?

● How does positive praise and feedback affect a student's emotions and application to their work?

 TRY using the positive words from the **RESOURCE** on page 114 in your feedback.

Also, get students to consider this 'Where am I with my learning?' diagram as an important part of the positive feedback process and to encourage personal reflection and evaluation of their work:

FEED ME!

WHERE AM I?

WHERE DO I WANT TO GET TO?

HOW AM I GOING TO GET THERE?

WHAT AM I GOING TO DO ABOUT IT?

As you can see, it all ties in nicely with assessment for learning, target-setting and self-evaluation.

 There is a **RESOURCE** on page 114 based on positive feedback that you might like to use – print it out for your class. Just remember, the best feedback you can give a pupil is saying thank you for attending your lesson. After all, it's all UPS!

Resource from *Of Teaching, Learning and Sherbet Lemons* © Nina Jackson, Paul Wrangles, 2C

18

INSET DAY BLUES

Q WE HAVE AN INSET EVERY YEAR IN OUR SCHOOL, BUT I WOULD RATHER JUST HAVE TIME DO SOME CATCH-UP AND MARKING. WHAT SHOULD I DO?

A Marking and catch-up takes up so much time, doesn't it? And there is never enough time to do it all. However, you might be lucky – maybe your next INSET will be on how to reduce your marking load and develop your time management skills!

There have been many changes to how the teaching profession views CPD and INSET over the years. Due to the pressures of marking, reporting, recording and accountability for standards, planning, preparation and assessment (PPA) time has been made statutory so teachers have non-contact time for marking and preparation.

As far as I'm concerned, continuing professional development – or, as some schools like to call it now, professional learning – is crucial for us as practitioners, as long as it serves to make us even better at what we do. What's more, effective, impactful teachers also have to be learners. I love to take responsibility for my own professional and personal learning by asking myself what I could be better at and what it is I need to know, understand and develop to support the ever-changing needs of our 21st century learners.

Whether we seek improved skills to enhance classroom performance, new roles in management, a better understanding of curriculum developments or the latest work in our subject areas, teachers need CPD. Lifelong learning is de rigueur in many fields of employment, so, surely, if any vocation should embrace the concept it is the teaching profession. I know I try my best – and that's an honest comment.

A colleague of mine once observed that CPD is the new 'learning deodorant'. I looked at him with a puzzled expression. He replied, 'It's the thing that keeps you fresh and zingy in the classroom. New ideas, seeing things from a different perspective and trying out new ideas learned from others.' So, hail the learning deodorant — at least it will stop the learning from having a stale, unpleasant aroma!

Schools have a duty to provide professional development for staff. This is something they must address to move education forward and skill up practitioners, as well as enabling us to pass on new ideas and methodologies to our pupils. Well-crafted, well-delivered CPD which is thought-provoking and stimulates a teacher's curiosity (the same as we want from our learners) is important because it delivers benefits to the individual, the profession and the pupils.

 THINK about these points:

- CPD/INSET ensures we can keep pace with the high standards of others in the teaching profession.

- CPD/INSET makes sure that we maintain and enhance the knowledge and skills we need to deliver a professional and invigorating learning experience for our pupils and the learning community as a whole.

- CPD/INSET guarantees that our professional knowledge stays relevant and up to date, which helps *us* stay relevant and up to date. The pace of change is probably faster than it's ever been (although I get the feeling all generations of teachers say that!). If we stand still we will get left behind, as the currency of our knowledge and skills gradually declines.

- CPD/INSET assists us in making a meaningful contribution to our team and all the other teachers we work with. This assists us in advancing our careers and moving into new positions where we can lead, manage, influence, coach and mentor others, and do so knowledgeably. (Would you want to be managed by someone who hadn't learned anything new in years?)

- CPD/INSET helps us to stay both interested *and* interesting. I would never want to get out of the interesting zone myself, as life and teaching would both become so humdrum. Experience is great in a teacher, but it can sometimes mean that we repeat what we have done before. Focused CPD opens us up to new possibilities, knowledge and skills. I have learned so much from my own colleagues and then seen the ripple effect of sharing these new skills with others. We have a built-in need as human beings to show off to others new things we have learned – it's part of our 'Oh, look what I can do' DNA!

● CPD/INSET can deliver a deeper understanding of what it means to be a professional – wanting to develop lifelong skills for our learners – along with a greater appreciation of the implications and impacts of our work.

● CPD/INSET supports the advance of the body of knowledge and technology within our profession.

● CPD/INSET can ignite the flame to try new ideas and activities in learning, and bring passion to lessons. We are all human, and the teacher who delivers outstanding lessons every day, every week, every month doesn't exist. But the teacher who continually shows a willingness to embrace new ideas and strengthen their own arsenal with proven innovative teaching and learning techniques are the real winners in my eyes.

 As your query is about CPD/INSET and your own personal issue is with time and marking, you might want to **TRY** these approaches to catching up and marking as an additional support guide, just to ease your workload:

● Prioritise your catch-up jobs by labelling them as 'urgent', 'soon' or 'can wait', and just 'trash' some jobs that are non-essential. If the job has been in your waiting queue for two weeks and no one has asked you about it, should you trash it? It's your call!

● Use technology to help you respond to pupils' work through audio annotation. Not everything has to have a grade or a mark. You may want to use some audio tools such as Audioboom or Notability to assist you with this. It's a quick and easy way of recording your thinking and giving feedback – and it will reach your SEND pupils too.

● The most effective forms of pupil feedback can take place through a personal learning dialogue. The pupils should know:

　■ Where they are at.

　■ Where they need to get to.

　■ How they are going to get there.

　■ What they are going to do about it.

■ Who or what is needed to help them get there.

● Consider some peer assessment strategies instead of traditional marking. Give the pupils the criteria for marking and ask them to assess each other's work in class. It will also help them to understand how their responses link with the original learning objectives. You may want to check out Jim Smith's *The Lazy Teacher's Handbook*, which is full of lazy but brilliant ways of tackling areas that you may be worried about.[1]

● Meet up with other teachers and if they also feel that marking or time management is an issue, set up your own professional learning network. Working together on a problem means that you pool your different approaches and come up with a solution.

To summarise, the right INSET at the right time and for the right reasons can be extremely powerful. And if it's not, then do something about it yourself. Remember, you can always use your own staff to run an INSET day. Take your inspiration from the format of the ever-popular TeachMeets or look to some of your students to lead staff training, especially in the area of digital technology.

Take responsibility for your own professional learning journey.

 There are **RESOURCES** on page 119 and 120 that you might like to use.

---

1   Jim Smith, *The Lazy Teacher's Handbook: How Your Students Learn More When You Teach Less* (Carmarthen: Crown House Publishing, 2010).

Self-evaluation CPD process

Key question 1. How is my CPD developing and enhancing:

- The learning in my classroom and pupil progress?
- My own professional skills?

Key question 2. How is my CPD developing my personal values and my professional commitment to:

- Contributing to the ethos of the school?
- Contributing to team effectiveness?
- Promoting a greater sense of identity among the wider school community?

Key question 3. How is my CPD developing my professional commitment with regards to:

- Improving pupils' learning?
- Improving my teaching?
- Improving the use of ICT inside and outside the classroom?
- Appropriately setting challenging targets?
- Tracking pupils to identify those who are 'at risk'?

Key question 4. How is my CPD developing my professional knowledge and understanding with regards to:

- Making a greater contribution to the school improvement plan?
- Making better use of evidence from my own evaluation and observations?
- The curriculum?
- Improving cross-curricular links for learning?
- Improving the motivation of learners?
- Ensuring differentiation is always the focus of inclusive learning?

NAME:		SCHOOL:			YEAR:
CPD development objective	CPD development activity	Date of activity	Duration		Outcome/impact on learning and teaching

Resource from *Of Teaching, Learning and Sherbet Lemons* © Nina Jackson, Paul Wrangles, 2015

19

MAKING CONNECTIONS – I + E = M

Q WHAT SHOULD I FOCUS ON TO GET MY STUDENTS MOTIVATED? I READ SOMEWHERE THAT IT'S ABOUT GETTING THE RELATIONSHIPS RIGHT, BUT IT MUST BE MORE THAN THAT.

A One of the biggest challenges we face as teachers is motivation. Not only do we have to consider motivating ourselves as practitioners, but also motivating our students both for learning and by the learning. This is paramount when it comes to embracing an ever-changing curriculum and achieving learning goals linked with personal aspirations.

During my first year of teaching, I remember a very humorous young boy saying to me, 'Ew is new, aren't ew? Well, I is tellin' ew one ffing now like ... I dun do writin', I doos drums!' It has stayed with me for over 25 years. Now that's what I call knowing what motivates a child to learn – drums! And not writing. Well, this particular child anyway.

There are two types of motivation:

1. **Intrinsic** – what internally motivates us as individuals.
2. **Extrinsic** – the way external factors motivate us.

Simple really – intrinsic + extrinsic = motivation (or I + E = M). Both types of motivation have an impact in our lessons, on discipline in and out of the classroom, and on engagement and achievement. Understanding motivation is only one aspect though. We also need to understand what causes a lack of motivation in our lessons. I have seen many teachers accidentally demotivate motivated learners by poorly planned and poorly delivered lessons.

So, before you begin to create your list of 101 great motivational tips for learning and engagement, reflect on what I consider to be the most crucial aspect of motivation in your classroom – getting to know your students.

Mutual knowing and learning relationships are key to learner happiness and personal development, which is why this is relevant to intrinsic motivation. This is especially true if you are working with SEND children. You need to know them and understand them; if not, your teacher tasks and activities will never meet their individual needs.

A well-organised, secure, safe and creative classroom, one in which your students know where things are, will generate a feeling of support for learning, and this, in turn, will help to motivate them as they prepare for each task. An unknown learning space can be a stressful environment for some students. If the classroom is well-thought-out, with a variety of resources, working spaces and opportunities to move around the room, this will encourage quality learning and a freedom to explore. Trust and independence also play an important part in supporting motivational attitudes to learning.

Your students come in all shapes and sizes, with different personality types and learning needs, which you will need to address as part of your overall curriculum planning. There will be some who love an audience and will have their vocal volume switch set permanently at 11, while others will choose to be on mute, but they all perform best when you give appropriate and individual praise. It is often the quiet learners who get overlooked, and it is these students who are in need of your personal support and attention through praise and reassurance. By all means embrace learner differences and attitudes to different types of teaching methodologies, but always make sure you set high learning expectations so they are all challenged.

As a forward-thinking teacher and practitioner, you will have to make the judgement on whether or not to have a classroom seating plan. I never used a strict plan myself, but allowed the students to mix and match their learning areas depending on their state of mind during a particular day. They chose who was the right person to sit next to or, indeed, their special individual learning space. But, for some teachers, a seating plan is essential. (I'm not here to judge anyone – they work for some, and not for others.) Either way, what matters most is that you are getting the best out of your learners.

One thing I am quite clear about is the need for effective and appropriate strategies to ensure that you do not dedicate all your time to the 'vocamax' students at the expense of the others. Coaching and mentoring support is key to learner development. Seating the vocamax students near your desk means not only that you get no peace, but also being close to you all the time may actually feed their 'vocahabit'. Furthermore, the other students may see this as you rewarding their attention-seeking behaviour with your time. Variety is indeed the spice of life, so make sure you have a good mix of students around you and near you.

With so many diverse learning needs in your classroom, please remember that one size most definitely does not fit all – and here I'm referring to worksheets (often the bane of a teacher's life!). If you are going to use worksheets, then make sure you include differentiated tasks. You do not need to create multiple worksheets – the art is in the content and methodology, not in the number of worksheets.

For some learners, especially students with special educational needs and disabilities, worksheets are a poor motivational tool and can be one of the biggest turn-offs to learning. Instead, consider setting tasks that can be completed orally. Oral responses, particularly when recorded on a digital device and then transcribed, can be truly magical, especially if you have iPads and use the built-in microphone to record students' responses. The iPad will then cleverly transcribe the oral recording into text – now that's a motivational tool in itself, especially if you activate the 'Speak Selection' in Settings/ Accessibility, as the students can then hear what they have recorded and read the text at the same time. Alternatively, if you are using older iPad models, you might want to use the Dragon Dictate app. You will need Wi-Fi in your classroom for this to work, or ask the learning/teaching assistant to write down the students' responses.

For the more able/gifted and talented students, ensure they are stretched by great enrichment activities, and not another add-on worksheet. As you develop your learning and personal relationships with your students, you will know what motivates them and what doesn't – it might be an individual research task for one student or becoming a learner buddy for another. But, for these children, enrichment is the key to keeping them engaged and motivated. A stagnant learner is a bored learner, and a bored learner is one who turns off the learning switch quicker than you can say 'Southern Electric!'

Students catch on quickly if they always get a certain coloured worksheet denoting their category of ability – it's one of the most damning things you can ever do to a child. In addition, others in the class will begin to identify who is able and who has SEND or is of lower academic ability. Don't forget, every child has a gift of one type or another, and it's your job to celebrate that gift and keep the motivational aspect of learning at its peak.

All of your students require a range of learning experiences, and the need for praise and reward is part of that diversity. It's about a learning dialogue between you and the student, no matter how small. Remember, small steps make big footprints in the snow! Always look for something positive in their work, their attitude to learning, their personal attainment and/or their achievement. And use strategies that will enable students to see and hear improvement. The smallest amount of personal attainment and achievement for a SEND student can be as momentous as the sizable progress made by a more academic student. It's all relevant and personal, but it's so often irrelevant and impersonal when we don't get it right. That is what makes learning so interesting – we all do it at different times and at different speeds.

If students feel they are constantly failing and not achieving, they will turn their focus on to something else, probably the latest blockbusting computer game, who kissed who at the weekend or, even worse, you will end up with classroom management and discipline issues. Remember that praise to criticism should be in the ratio of four to one. Also bear in mind that you need to make pupils responsible for themselves, so show them you trust them. This two-way relationship model will motivate even the most unengaged learners.

 THINK about these questions:

- What steps do I need to take to address motivation in my classroom?
- How do I know what motivates the learners I teach?
- Why are some of my learners not motivated?
- Where and how can I gather information to help me motivate my learners?
- What does motivation look like and feel like?
- What strategies do I use to motivate myself that I could share with my learners?

 TRY using the four elements of motivation:

1. Engagement – as a teacher, show that you are interested in every pupil's work and value them as an individual, regardless of their needs, attainment, behaviour or character.

2. Structure – determine an effective structure through different and engaging learning experiences. It's about finding the balance between authoritarian control and pupils' self-determination in the learning experience.

3. Stimulation – use activities, tasks and opportunities that engage pupils' interests. For example, create a 'wall of wonder' and ask the pupils to write on it about what motivates them in their learning. This would be a very quick way of engaging them in reflection about their experiences, as well as collaborating and sharing ideas and stimuli.

4. Feedback – this needs to be constructive, supportive and emotionally uplifting to one and all. This will not only help with progression but it will also give them the feel-good factor. And, as we know, anyone who has the feel-good factor often rises to any challenge set before them!

You might also want to consider using a 'motivation bank' of key words and phrases. Here's a starting point, but add yours to it too:

- Thank you
- Awesome
- Brilliant
- Fabulous
- Loved it!
- Tip-top
- Wow – I was blown away ...
- You exceeded my expectations, just amazing
- Super
- Smashing
- Great
- How did you do that? You *must* tell me, I was so excited by your work and the content – just marvellous
- Now add your own ...

The use of differentiated language is crucial, depending on your audience, and the key to this is putting passion in your voice when giving verbal feedback. To produce a similar effect in written feedback you could try using emojis. Emojis are similar to emoticons, smileys or ideograms and were first used in electronic messages in Japan, although they are now found on electronic devices across the world. The word emoji means 'picture' (e) + 'character' (moji). Here are some of the common ones:

:-)   :-(:-0   :-\

Emojis can be used as part of written feedback or as motivational icons around the classroom. You could even get your pupils to create some of their own emojis – now that's a thought!

 Use the **RESOURCE** on page 127 to improve motivation.

INTRINSIC

+ EXTRINSIC

MOTIVATION!

Resource from *Of Teaching, Learning and Sherbet Lemons* © Nina Jackson, Paul Wrangles, 2015

20

THE DEATH OF A PARENT

Q ONE OF MY STUDENTS LOST A PARENT RECENTLY. DO YOU HAVE ANY IDEAS WHEN IT COMES TO SUPPORTING HER?

A Saying sorry doesn't and won't even begin to help your student. Her world has been torn apart and may have left her with the deepest of wounds and scars which will never heal fully. The wounds may become fainter, but they will never go away. Sometimes, when we don't know what else to say, we often say sorry. It's not ideal but at least it's something. (The most ridiculous thing for anyone to say is, 'I feel your pain …' No, you don't. No one can feel the pain of another human being. You can only empathise or sympathise.) There is no script for grieving or knowing how to cope, or not cope. And why should anyone need to cope during such a traumatic life experience?

This is one of the most difficult issues a teacher might face in their career. I am not a grievance counsellor, but I am an experienced teacher and human being with an open heart and a listening ear. Having been in a similar situation when one of my students lost a parent, I can only reach out to you and give you as much advice as I feel I can.

 To start with, here are some things to **THINK** about:

- Make sure that you (or another teacher or the head teacher) tell the other children about the death of the student's parent. Step in before tongues begin wagging or Chinese whispers invent or distort the truth.

- Communicate with the family and ask them what they would like you to say to other students so there is no conflict with their wishes.

- Do not be afraid of the words 'dead' or 'death'. Often, we feel that choosing other words might be easier, but easier for who – us or the child?

- Worrying about finding the right words is better than taking the coward's way out, which is saying and doing nothing. Something is always better than nothing; even a gentle touching of the arm may help when you really don't have the words.

- If a child grips on to you or needs a hug, then let it happen. Offering 'safeness' and simply holding the child may be their only source of comfort at that moment in time.

- Ensure that the school and the children send messages of condolence to the family. This is really important. Ignoring a death because you don't know what to say is not acceptable.

- We all need honesty in our lives. Children and young people going through bereavement need it even more so. It's always better to answer difficult and awkward questions with the truth. You do yourself and the child a complete injustice if you don't.

- Always allow the child to express their emotions and feelings in their own way. Reassure them that it's okay to respond in that way and encourage them to grieve however feels natural for them. After all, we are all the same, but we are so different. Remember that it's fine for you to share your own emotions and feelings of sadness with the child as well. It's natural and human.

- Be a listener, over and over and over again, because sometimes it is what a grieving child needs the most. And I don't just mean in the days and weeks following the bereavement – it may take months or years.

- Give the child space, time and an unconditional support network of people in school to help. This network means everyone. I once saw a child sitting on a stairway with Jenny, my classroom cleaning lady. There they were sharing a biscuit and a cup of tea, and the child had a yellow duster in her hand. The little girl said she couldn't find me for tea and a chat, so she thought she'd ask Jenny if she could sit with her instead. They couldn't find tissues as my office was locked, so Jenny found the next best thing, the yellow duster! It was quite a lovely moment. We didn't move to 'proper' chairs – sitting there together on the stairs with tea and biscuits just seemed the right thing to do at that time.

- When a child needs to talk, or just be, find someone and somewhere that's appropriate for them. Make it right for them. Be there for them their way. End of.

- Remember the parent who is grieving too. If they contact you or want to come into the school and be with the child, then make sure there are opportunities for this to happen. It might be for just 10 minutes or it might be for most of the day. They need people around them who will just be accepting of whatever is required at that particular time, and knowing there are other adults looking out for their child will mean so much to them.

- When children and adults are grieving, their world is just that at the time – their world. It is distorted and even broken, but knowing they can just be the way they need to be is incredibly helpful, so help them to experience this.

- Always make sure there is plenty of tea, coffee and biscuits, and maybe even a soft blanket to hold if they need it. Sitting together under a blanket can create a safe place, especially if the fabric pulls them closer together and they are enclosed within it. As strange as this might seem for some people, strange is the norm at these times.

- We all react to trauma and grief in different ways. Do not assume that a lack of emotion or reaction means the child does not care. It may be that the reality of the parent's death has not sunk in yet. Some young people believe they need to demonstrate that they're 'coping' (whatever that may look or sound like) because it's a sign of maturity.

- Never judge. Grief is personal and every child or adult will do it in their own way. There isn't a plaster for that, you know!

- Talk about the dead person. Talk about memories. The bereaved child may well need and want to do this. Ignoring the dead parent can be perceived as a denial that they ever existed, so talking about them with the child can mean the world.

- Offer comfort and reassurance that they are not responsible for what has happened and could not have prevented it. It's very common for young children to feel that they have in some way been the cause of the death, so do all you can to reassure them.

- Be sensitive to events such as Mother's Day and Father's Day in school. Make sure your teaching staff know who might be affected.

 TRY to make sure the school:

- Has a clear understanding of how to support the child and the parent – it's about a caring dialogue.

● Is flexible in every way with regards to the needs of the parent and child, even if it means going to the park for the afternoon and having an ice cream together, because it's the right thing to do at that given moment. Be flexible with their emotions and needs – that is one of the greatest gifts you can give.

● Talks about death openly in school in general. Grieving for the first time can be an almighty blow to our world.

● Has a whole school bereavement policy

Remember that nothing prepares us for the passing of a loved one, even if we know it's coming.

On page 133 you'll find a **RESOURCE** which may prove useful.

Here's another **RESOURCE** that might help. Ian Gilbert's *The Little Book of Bereavement for Schools* (Carmarthen: Crown House Publishing, 2010), written with his three children, Will, Olivia and Phoebe, offers a very personal perspective on what schools could and should be doing after the death of a parent. This book should be in every school across the world.

I hope my suggestions can help your student and I hope that you can embrace what is needed in your school. Do let me know how things go, won't you?

HOW CAN I GET OVER IT?
HOW CAN I EVER BE STRONG?
WHY IS DEATH SO CRUEL?
HOW WILL I EVER MOVE ON?

TIME ALONE AND TIME TO GRIEVE
THAT'S WHAT I NEED FOR THIS
PLEASE DON'T RUSH ME, TIME STANDS STILL
MY HEART NEEDS HEALING, SO, SO ILL

I'VE CRIED AND CRIED, SO MANY TEARS
THOSE TEARS OF LOVE AND LOSS
I MAY NOT EVER TRULY HEAL
FROM DEATH, FROM GRIEF AND HOW I FEEL

YOU'LL KNOW WHEN I AM READY
YOU'LL KNOW WHEN I AM STRONG
BUT LEAVE ME NOW FOR TIME I NEED
THE SCARS, THE HURT, MY HEART DOTH BLEED

AND WHEN THE TIME IS RIGHT FOR ME
TO SHARE MY GRIEF WITH YOU AND THEE
YOU'LL KNOW, I'LL COME AND TELL YOU WHY
I'VE FINALLY BEEN ABLE TO SAY GOODBYE

TO THE ONE I LOVE.

Resource from *Of Teaching, Learning and Sherbet Lemons* © Nina Jackson, Paul Wrangles, 2015

21

SHE DOESN'T LIKE ME

Q I DON'T THINK MY LINE MANAGER LIKES ME VERY MUCH. SHE NEVER DELEGATES ANYTHING MY WAY OR COMES INTO MY LESSONS. WHAT SHOULD I DO?

A Working in education means we need to have a professional approach towards our colleagues and a positive attitude to the privilege of teaching young people. Relationships might just revolve around our work, but it's always nice to get on well with our colleagues on a personal level too. Which is why it can be all the more concerning when you get the impression that a colleague doesn't like you. I'm sure this won't be the first time you've felt like this, and I can promise you it won't be the last!

So, with that in mind, let's get one thing straight: professionals do not need to like each other in order to respect each other's professionalism. Occasionally, we have the pleasure of working with people we really like, respect and respond to. And even better, they like, respect and respond to us. The icing on the cake!

However, when these factors are not present and the relationship isn't so great, this can have an emotional impact on the way we deal with these individuals. At times, this makes us afraid to approach them in case they make us feel undervalued. This, in turn, makes us feel all the more vulnerable to their potentially negative responses. And when that person is your line manager then things get even more complicated, both inside and outside your own head. However, don't forget that there are others in the school you can approach to talk about this if need be.

THINK about this question: do you believe your line manager is an ineffective manager or just an unpleasant person (in your eyes, be honest)?

135

You may feel your line manager is ineffective if she does not give you the direction, support and guidance you need to succeed at your job. If so, consider what specific areas you want or need to develop as a practitioner that you know she will be able to assist you with. Often, a little psychological mind game of making others feel they are wanted and valued can produce great results. They may believe that they have the upper hand when it comes to your professional development, but you know that it is your hand at play – gaining her curiosity and interest and making her feel good in the process.

If your line manager is unpleasant towards you, then you may need to consider whether you can tell her that she is making you uncomfortable or explain why her manner is unfriendly. She may not even be aware that she is being that disagreeable – she may think she is just being assertive. However, if it seems personal or you feel professionally undervalued, this can feel like a form of bullying, so it's in your best interest to point this out in a very calm and thoughtful manner. She may even thank you for it as she may actually be upset that this is how she is making you feel. It's always better to be open and honest, as difficult as it may be for you to pluck up the courage to say so.

It is up to you to create a clear plan and structure of what you require from her as part of her job. Be clear on what you want to achieve and the support you require from her. This will mean a concise plan of action if you are going to make any headway. The key point to remember is that your main purpose is to build the professional aspect of your relationship, with the hope of productive future learning dialogues. You don't need to see eye to eye personally, but you do need to be involved in brain-to-brain thinking in order to develop your pedagogical practice.

 Here's something else for you to **THINK** about. You might not like it, but an honest person needs to ask it of themselves occasionally: do you think you (or your thinking) might be the problem? Could it be that the fact you *think* she doesn't like you is clouding your judgement about her role as your line manager?

Take a step back and answer these questions truthfully:

- What are you doing to help yourself?
- Are you attempting to develop an effective working relationship with your line manager? Have you asked for regular professional meetings to review your work and the work of your students?

- Is there an agenda for your meetings? If so, who writes the minutes? (I suggest you keep notes of 'formal' professional meetings.)

- How are you ensuring that she supports you and guides you with the strategic work of the departmental or school plan?

- Does she come into your lessons to see what the children are learning? Have you asked her to? If not, take a big step and do so. If not you then perhaps the children can ask so that she can observe the progress they are making.

- Have you clearly told your line manager that you would like some extra responsibility to develop your professional portfolio and practice? Could she think that by not delegating to you she is doing you a favour?

So, take a deep breath and remember that everyone is the hero of their own story, and everyone believes they are the party in the right. Your line manager is no different. As hard as this may be, ask yourself honestly if you are contributing to the poor relationship. Take a moment to reflect.

If you know, and can show, that you are being unfairly treated, then take a confident step towards doing something about it. Have you actually asked her why she doesn't come into your lessons or delegate work to you? If not, then now is the time. Remember, you are no circus monkey, and having to capture someone's attention does not a wonderful relationship make. It's about unravelling the issues, if there are any. She may not feel there is a problem, so talk to her first.

 I also want you to think about the following and **TRY** to put some of the suggestions into action. This will help you to get the balance right, professionally and personally.

- Manage your obvious need for your line manager to see you in action by making formal requests for visits to lessons. Give her an overview of what the prior learning was and where you hope to take the next learning adventure. Think of this as sharing pre-learning, present learning and post-learning opportunities.

- Once you've made a formal request for some lesson visits, and these have taken place, ask for some feedback. This can be either verbal or written, but it will enable you to develop a healthier working relationship with your manager. This will be good for both of you.

- Ask your line manager, informally at first, if you could visit some of her lessons to observe the teaching and learning, as you feel this would be an invaluable opportunity to see someone teaching in a different way and learn from her expertise. She should be very pleased that you are asking to watch her teach. You are now setting the scene for networked learning and professional development.

- Share examples of work by the children with her. Perhaps get the children to video their learning progress so that it feels as if it is coming from them, not just from you.

 If the relationship is causing you real stress and anxiety, **TRY** the following:

- Aim to unravel what you are really concerned about. Is it her failure to communicate with you, a lack of appreciation of your work or a combination of both?

- Take time for yourself during the day to reflect on your work and celebrate the impact you have had on the pupils' learning.

- Keep a professional work diary or paper trail of interactions with your manager. This can be a great way of recording your own achievements. If there is no time to share them with your manager, you can at least show her parts of your professional diary. Writing down how you feel, as well as your achievements, can be very powerful too. This also means that if, in the future, the professional relationship breaks down then you will have the evidence to share. If you want to keep it as a private journal or diary, then this is also an excellent way for you to be very honest with yourself about your feelings and professional judgements.

- Talk is good, so think about asking someone else to be your professional mentor, or even just find a colleague with whom you can share aspirations and teaching and learning strategies. Shadowing someone who is in a position of responsibility which you aspire to can be a useful way of sharing ideas. A mentor will help you to see different management and leadership strategies, which will include working with difficult people.

- If your line manager's main problem is that she doesn't communicate well with you or fails to set you performance goals (which she should be doing as part of your professional development), take the first step and ask her what professional priorities she has for you. Some managers like others in their team to instigate communication so that they can measure their enthusiasm for change and professional development, as well as their accountability.

● Meeting regularly, even if it's just for 10 minutes or so, will allow you to build a more communicative professional relationship. It doesn't matter whether you 'like' each other or not – it's the professional dialogue about learning and teaching that counts.

● Try the technique of 'managing up' and give constructive criticism about professional issues – but try not to sound condescending or cocky. You are both professional adults and this can be a good way of beginning a healthy interaction. You might even have the confidence to tell your manager that you feel you are being slightly neglected from a professional perspective. She might not even realise this – unless you use the unsubtle 'custard pie in your face' technique and really tell her how you feel (which is not to be recommended!).

● Be armed with suggestions that you believe might improve the relationship. Use questions like, 'How can we ...?' or 'What should we do about ...'? By using 'we' it shows you are seeing the challenge as a joint thinking task.

● If things really are that bad, then seek advice from a senior manager and talk to them honestly about your professional concerns, outlining the fact that you are not being observed or given the opportunity to work as a team. There will be aspects of her managerial role that she should be delivering, and that includes observing your lessons, discussing professional development and being accountable for the learning and teaching in your lessons.

So, to sum up, continue doing the good work you are already doing with your pupils, and celebrate and share the learning with your line manager. Ask formally for her to come into your lessons, either to chat with the pupils about their learning or to do a lesson observation. Don't turn yourself into an attention-seeker – just take the professional steps involved in sharing as much with her as you can. In return, ask for her response, support and guidance.

 There's a **RESOURCE** on page 140 for you to consider using. It's a professional learning plan that you can complete and discuss with your line manager.

🪪 Name:	🛡 School:	📅 Date:
	✴ Specialism:	📅 School week:

💭 **Learning to be celebrated:**

🔍 **Evidence:**

🎯 **Targets for improvement:**

❓ **Professional questions:**

🧑‍🤝‍🧑 **Support, guidance and coaching needed:**

📖 **Learning and teaching references and literature to share:**

🤝 **Meetings/discussions arranged with line manager:**

🕐 **Date/Time:**

💭 **Weekly reflection:**

22

WHERE'S THE SPARK GONE?

Q I'VE GOT A CLASS WHO ARE REALLY QUIET. I WISH THEY WEREN'T SO INTROVERTED AND HAD A BIT MORE SPARK! WHAT CAN I DO?

A We are who we are. I am who I am, just as you are who you are. And the pupils in your classrooms, well, they are who they are. Our individual personalities play a part in everything we do or choose not to do. In particular, our levels of introversion and extroversion have far-reaching effects on our lives, including everything from the language we use to our risk-taking behaviours and our mental health to our happiness.

It may be that you have just the right number of introverts in your class to create a critical mass that makes the whole class quiet. Or, and you need to be honest here, they may not be sparky enough for you because the lesson content, learning environment and access to diverse, engaging learning activities just are not there. Are you waiting for them to provide the catalyst when it should be coming from you? When it comes to thinking in terms of introverts and extroverts, bear in mind that introverts can be sparky too – they just show it in other ways. Sparks are not always measured by a volume switch, you know!

It's also worth reflecting on what you mean by sparky – after all, we all have our own view on what 'a bit more spark' means. One teacher's sparky class is another teacher's noisy class. If what you're seeking is a more energetic class, full of children's voices, chit-chat and buzz, then create activities which get them making noise and sounds or get them involved in calling out, shouting answers, celebrating learning with heckles and other noise-based responses.

Do not attempt to change the personalities of the individual pupils just because they are a quiet class – some teachers would give their left arm to have that class!

THINK about the following questions:

- Are they quiet because you are loud?
- Are they quiet because they are bored?
- Are they quiet because they have switched off from learning?
- Are they quiet because they are fearful of you?
- Are they quiet in every lesson?
- Are they quiet outside your lessons?
- Are they only quiet at certain times?
- Do you know what sparks their curiosity?
- Do you know what gets them excited?
- Do you know what turns them on to learning and what turns them off?
- Do you hear them laughing in your lessons?
- Have you ever told them they can shout as loud as they want – if they want to?
- Do you tell them that they are a super class and you believe in every one of them?
- Have you thought about making and creating a sparky lesson, full of exciting activities and learning experiences – *after* you have asked the pupils what ignites their interest?

Did you know that in terms of language and oracy, extroverts and introverts speak differently? This is sometimes matched by the speed in which they talk and express themselves. According to a study in the *Journal of Language and Social Psychology*, the language of extraverts includes high levels of abstraction while introverts are more likely to stick to concrete facts.[1]

At least one-third of us are introverts. They are the ones who prefer listening to speaking, who innovate and create but dislike self-promotion, and who favour working on their own over working in teams. Did you know that Rosa Parks, Chopin, Dr Seuss (Theodor Seuss Geisel) and Charles Darwin could all be classed as introverts, and who

---

1 See Camiel J. Beukeboom, Martin Tanis and Ivar E. Vermeulen, The Language of Extraversion: Extraverted People Talk More Abstractly, Introverts Are More Concrete, *Journal of Language and Social Psychology* 32(2) (2013): 191–201.

wouldn't want these people in their class? I am often extremely jealous of introverts as I could learn so much from their thoughtful timely thinking, rather than my usual 'bull in a china shop' type responses.

It's such a shame that many of our schools and workplaces are designed around extroverts, mainly because of the belief that collaboration is the key to creativity and productivity, even though the opposite is true for introverts. I love working with my introvert colleagues – they are some of the greatest educational thinkers of the 21st century. They seem to have an incredible gift for listening to others, digesting information and developing their own creative thinking by sharing it in some amazing books.

Extroverts (like me!) have a great deal to learn from introverts. Personally, I have discovered that my life is better when there is a good balance of both sorts of behaviour. This affords me greater mental happiness and the ability to unravel some of the supersonic 'Ninja thinking' that I have at times – slowing down this process so that I don't blurt out my first answer (often one that doesn't make much sense!). Learning to listen to others and thinking carefully about what they are saying can be an exhilarating experience. Sparky, but quietly sparky!

Remember, too, what I keep coming back to: we are all the same and yet we are all different. One concern about pigeonholing different personalities and attitudes to learning is that it can be harmful to those who feel they don't fit in or are unappreciated. For example, extroverts are often gregarious individuals – a 'people person'. In societies like our own this outlook is highly valued, which in turn can make introverts feel as if something is wrong with them. This can start them on a negative spiral of unhappiness and further introversion, which is not something we want for our pupils and learners.

I strongly believe that if we consider what we really mean by sparky learners, then it does not imply that each and every classroom, activity and experience needs to be a Disney World parade, an all-singing, all-dancing showcase of educational entertainment and hilarity. It's important to remember that thoughtful, intense and quiet learning can be one of the most powerful ways to engage the thinking brain and experience deep learning. This can also be embedded in assessment for learning procedures by carefully monitoring, evaluating and reviewing our students' learning and thinking.

We all need different learning experiences, and it may be that you meet the learning needs of this particular class by considering more reflective ways of sparking their learning.

TRY to:

● Ask the pupils what sparks their interest and how they would prefer to share their learning with you.

● Provide a range of learning experiences within one activity (which any good teacher should be doing anyway – differentiation and inclusion and all that!) and let them tell you why that is their chosen method of learning.

● Accept, expect and respect that this class will show their sparky learning in their chosen way. It doesn't have to be full of explosive fireworks.

● Develop new techniques for yourself as a teacher that will allow you to coach and mentor individual pupils, developing a deeper learning relationship with them rather than expecting to see visual or aural responses instantly.

● Give introverted pupils written tasks through which they can think and present their ideas.

● Use technology to your advantage. Introverts often feel at ease with a digital device because they don't necessarily have to speak out loud or share their thinking immediately. They need time to consider, decipher and collate what are their best and most advanced answers from a plethora of ideas. This is what I call the marrying of the thinking brain with the digital brain.

● Try to mould your own personality to that of the pupils you are working with (not the other way round). Just because someone is quiet does not mean they are passive. As a child, Gandhi used to love to run home after school where he would sit alone, revise his thinking from the day and then use his inner passion to generate his own ideas. From there his natural leadership qualities emerged. Surely, Gandhi would be classed as a calm but energised spark, wouldn't he? He hated the hustle and bustle of being around people, and felt that he needed to be alone to analyse the world and its problems in a quiet, reflective space. You might like to think about Gandhi when meeting with your class next. It's the quiet sparks who can fuel the most creative of thinking in the extrovert sparks.

Here are some other things to **THINK** about:

● Judge no one for the personality they have.

● Judge no one for wearing a different type of thinking veil.

- Judge no one for their silent thoughts, for they are the most powerful and personal of all.
- Judge no one for being the same as everyone else, but different too.
- Judge no one for not putting their hand up or calling out the answer in class, for they may well be answering in a different manner.
- Judge yourself if you only use the hands-up method and no other strategies for eliciting responses.
- Judge yourself if you are not giving your pupils different learning experiences.
- Judge only those who have committed the absolute sin of unacceptable teaching and learning, which is to not consider the needs of all the different types of pupils we have in our care.
- Praise yourself for asking questions about the different types of learning sparks that we have in our classrooms.
- Praise yourself for reading this response to your question, for you are on a quest to support the needs of all your pupils.
- Praise all your learners in the right way for the smallest amount of progress they make.

On page 146 is a **RESOURCE** you can use in your classroom to help bring in a bit of spark.

If you want an amazing **RESOURCE** that can support sparky learning, why not invest in *365 Things To Make You Go Hmmm …* by Sparky Teaching (Carmarthen: Independent Thinking Press, 2014) (@sparkyteaching). And check out the website www.sparkyteaching.com for lots of sparky thinking and learning ideas for every child, introvert or otherwise.

WHAT MAKES YOU GO 'HMMM ...'?

SHOULD YOU CARE MORE ABOUT DOING THE RIGHT THING

OR DOING THINGS RIGHT?

WHAT HAPPENS AFTER WE DIE?

IF YOU COULD SEND A MESSAGE TO EVERY WORLD LEADER

WHAT WOULD YOU SAY TO THEM?

WHAT WOULD YOU DO IF YOU KNEW YOU COULDN'T FAIL?

HOW DOES YOUR LEARNING FIZZ?

WHO TAUGHT BIRDS TO STAMP THE GROUND TO IMITATE RAIN?

WHICH PERIOD IN HISTORY WOULD YOU MOST LIKE TO HAVE LIVED IN?

WHAT MAKES A SPARKY TEACHER?

WOULD YOU RATHER BE ABLE TO MAKE NEW MEMORIES

OR LOSE ALL THE MEMORIES YOU ALREADY HAVE?

Resource from *Of Teaching, Learning and Sherbet Lemons* © Nina Jackson, Paul Wrangles, 201

23

DYSGRAPHIA – MORE THAN JUST BAD HANDWRITING

Q I HAVE SOME CHILDREN WHOSE HANDWRITING IS ALMOST ILLEGIBLE, AND I DON'T WANT TO EMBARRASS THEM BY SAYING THEIR WORK IS BAD. CAN YOU HELP ME WITH SOME TIPS, PLEASE? MY SENCO SAYS THEY MIGHT HAVE DYSGRAPHIA AS THEY HAVE OTHER SPECIAL EDUCATIONAL NEEDS AS WELL. I'M NOT SURE I REALLY KNOW WHAT DYSGRAPHIA IS, SO ANY HELP WOULD BE MUCH APPRECIATED.

A Too many of us in education respond to dysgraphia by dismissing it as a handwriting issue, whereas actually it is often associated with other special educational needs – or learning differences as you know I like to call them. Once we acknowledge this as a problem, we can work on supporting these pupils with guidance, alternative methods of producing their work and, most importantly, giving them the emotional support they need to reassure them that, despite their problems with handwriting, they can still be high achieving individuals.

In a nutshell, dysgraphia is a neurological disorder linked with significant motor or sensory-motor challenges, such as poor handwriting, problems with spelling and difficulties in getting thoughts down on paper. 'Dys' means 'difficulty' and 'graphia' relates to 'writing'. Dysgraphia has been linked with neurological trauma in childhood, as well as physical impairments such as Tourette's syndrome, attention deficit disorder (ADD) and attention deficit hyperactivity disorder (ADHD), learning differences such as dyslexia and autistic spectrum disorders such as Asperger's syndrome, although it doesn't mean they are necessarily directly linked. In the *Diagnostic and Statistical*

Manual of Mental Disorders, dysgraphia is described as a 'disorder of written expression',[1] meaning that an individual's writing skills are substantially below those expected for their age, as measured by intelligence and educational background.

It is important to remember that having a neurological impairment does not mean there is an intellectual impairment. I have worked with some very special young people, highly gifted individuals, who only have dysgraphia problems and show no other evidence of SEND.

For a pupil with dysgraphia, it is writing that is the problem, not the ability to read or the thinking behind their writing. However, every pupil is an individual, so no two pupils will have identical symptoms. For this reason, it's essential that an appropriate test is carried out so that the education team, parents and support workers can ensure the best EHCP is in place for the pupil.

There are three main types of dysgraphia: dyslexic (characterised by illegible text when spontaneously written but normal when copied, and poor oral spelling), motor (both written and copied text are illegible due to poor motor skills) and spatial (both written and copied text are illegible due to a defect in understanding space). Dysgraphia is also linked with other learning differences which share similar coordination and word awareness difficulties.

It is also worth highlighting that stress can exacerbate dysgraphia. (Have you ever noticed that when you are overworked and tired, or have to take down notes really quickly, your handwriting dramatically changes and sometimes you can't even read your own writing? This will give you just a little glimpse into what it's like for a dyspgraphic child.) They know what they are writing, and it all seems fine to them at that moment, but then when you or they come to read it, it's like a spaghetti world of letters, shapes and doodles.

Many of the greatest creative thinkers are dysgraphics – Agatha Christie, Albert Einstein and Thomas Edison to name but a few. Our unique learning differences can be a boost to our creativity, forcing us to come at the world differently and therefore producing unusual results. After all, you don't get to choose the way you're put together; you just have to learn to know yourself and respond accordingly.

---

1   American Psychiatric Association, *Diagnostic and Statistical Manual of Mental Disorders, Fifth Edition (DSM-5)* (Arlington, VA: APA, 2013).

To help you with pupils who may have dysgraphia, here are some things to look out for and **THINK** about:

- Written text is sometimes unfinished – occasionally some letters may be missing.
- Speaking out loud while writing text.
- Finding it hard to select the right words and being unable to unravel thinking into written text.
- Anxiety about writing – sometimes plain refusing to.
- Shapes and letter sometimes don't make sense.
- Issues with holding a writing implement.
- Squiggles and doodles which the pupil sees as letters and shapes.
- Errors with spelling and incomplete sentences.
- Mixture of upper/lower case letters.
- Flowing lines of large text which look more like a drawing rather than specific letters.
- Holding the page upside down or at a strange angle in order to write.
- Loud noise/music or crowds of people sparks personal upset or emotional distress, which can lead to thinking becoming confused.
- Sensitivity to artificial light – so watch those light switches.
- Writing can at times cause pain in the wrist, hand or arm.
- Difficulty in working with lined or graph paper – that is, being unable to confine writing to certain spaces.
- Tiredness in school during the afternoon.
- Homework can be a real challenge because of the time spent trying to write.
- Needs support from a teaching assistant as a scribe – it which case it might be helpful to use an iPad to support the child in their learning.
- Their thinking and what they've written are not the same – it can become garbled at times.
- Difficulty in working independently and may fall behind with school tasks and assignments.

If your pupils are demonstrating any of these signs, then you, the school and the parents, need to make sure there is plenty of emotional support and encouragement available, as well as specific learning support. Some of the most successful tools we have to inspire learners are motivation, praise, confidence and encouragement, so let's make sure our students regularly have plenty of them. I am a great believer in feeding the heart to feed the brain.

 TRY these strategies and tips with your pupils.

HOLD THAT GRIP

If the pupil has difficulty gripping a writing instrument, then experiment with different pens or pencils, encourage proper grip and posture, and/or develop keyboarding skills to compensate.

You might want to try some of these: PenAgain ErgoSof Pen, triangular grip pen/pencil, Stubbi pencil grip or a Dexball writing aid.

GO LARGE WITH MOTOR MOVEMENT

If the pupil has difficulty remembering how to form letters, then reinforce letter formation with large motor movements, smaller hand/finger motions and multisensory reinforcements such as visual and auditory cues. Practise letters and sounds in lots of different ways (e.g. see it, hear it, say it, trace it with a body part) and find tricks to help the pupil remember letters. For example, for the correct direction of b and d, use your left hand to make a b and your right hand to make a d (it might look like a mirror image or a pair of glasses with horns!). I love tricks for learning – don't you? It's always the best way to remember things because tricks make smiles!

SPELLSEQUENCE

If the pupil has difficulty spelling or sequencing letters, use multisensory techniques to establish visual, auditory and motor memory. I like to use a brilliant app called Cursive – I'm addicted to it myself as it's such a fun, auditory way of developing the visual aspect of writing.

POWER THOUGHTS

If the student with dysgraphia has difficulty organising their thoughts, use the POWER approach to the writing process:[2]

Plan what you are going to write about.

Organise with idea maps or outlines.

Write your thoughts – if you can't get started with a blank page, start with an index or use a grid card.

Edit your own writing as well as have someone else edit your draft.

Revise your draft with your own and someone else's edits.

Additionally, help the student to find someone whose writing they really like and ask them to model how to get started. They might also want to use mind mapping apps or software – an app like MyScript Memo, which I use all the time, takes your own handwriting and changes it into text. Just brilliant!

POSITIVE POLLY NOT NEGATIVE NELLIE

If the pupil gets anxious about writing and has a critical voice in their head when writing, then help them to develop positive self-talk to respond to it.

---

2 POWER was originally developed by Simone Acosta and Regina G. Richards. See Cursive Writing: A Multisensory Approach, in California Consortium, *Resource Directory* (Baltimore, MD: International Dyslexia Association, 1999).

DIGITAL LEARNING FOR A LEARNING DIFFERENCE

If a pupil with dysgraphia can't get their ideas down on paper, they can record their responses in an audio format. With the AudioNote app, they can record then fast-forward through their ideas and stop the recording when an idea needs to be fleshed out. Other useful tools include the apps Dragon Dictate and Pages, or double tap the 'Fn' key on a MacBook keyboard to initialise the record your voice function, which will then notate the audio for you. Our world is a new world in which the thinking brain can merge with the digital brain.

 On page 153 you'll find a **RESOURCE** which gives advice on dealing with dysgraphia.

STRATEGIES AND CONSIDERATIONS IN SUPPORTING LEARNERS WITH Dysgraphia

VISUAL RESOURCES
- Pictures, photos, cards
- Videos
- Use of IT – iPad is best

COMMUNICATION SKILLS
- Trouble following instructions
- Getting thoughts onto paper an issue
- Get physically and mentally tired
- Plenty of support needed – emotionally and academic

FINE MOTOR SKILLS
- Handwriting issues
- May need special pens
- Digital device to help
- Difficulty with manipulation
- Gripping equipment painful
- Size of fonts
- Formation of text

GETTING ORGANISED
- Mind maps
- Checklists
- Vocabulary lists
- Time to read key words
- Planning map for homework
- Bullet points
- Time to plan
- Learning desk mats

CLASSROOM MANAGEMENT
- Audio recording of lessons
- Personal audio device – iPad is best
- Speech to text access
- Time to write
- Chunk the learning
- Syntax and grammar structure support

Resource from *Of Teaching, Learning and Sherbet Lemons* © Nina Jackson, Paul Wrangles, 2015

24

UNVEILING EVERY LEARNER'S INVISIBLE STAMP

Q I WANT THE BEST FOR MY CHILDREN, BUT OFTEN I'M NOT REALLY SURE WHAT SOME OF THEM ARE GOOD AT OR WHAT SKILLS OR TALENTS THEY HAVE. WHAT IF SOME DON'T HAVE ANY?

A Let me begin by telling you a story. My wonderful 96-year-old tadcu (that's the Welsh word for grandfather) once told me that we are all born with an 'invisible stamp'. He said that God gave us all something that we would be great at as we grow from babies into adulthood. He then told me that, as a teacher, it was my job to unveil this invisible stamp in every child. 'You see, Nina,' he said, 'I was born with the stamp of being a poet, your mother the stamp of being a nurse, and you the stamp of being a musician and teacher.'

Tadcu believes we all have different stamps and that with these stamps we come together as a human race and create a diverse world. Each stamp has its own place and fulfils different needs. Without these individual stamps we would all be the same and the world would not function. We need people with different stamps so that all our needs can be met. For me, this is a very thoughtful, wise and useful philosophy, and one that all teachers can benefit from.

The idea of unveiling every child's invisible stamp as part of my job as a teacher has remained with me for many years. I often share this with colleagues so they too can support pupils in finding their place in the world, helping them to discover what their talents could be – or might be if channelled in the right direction – and what gifts they naturally have but are not fully aware of, yet (which is where a gifted teacher comes in).

We are all good, and even great, at different things. These differences are what makes us individuals – they are part of our personality and make-up. Some people have talents and skills they don't even know they have, while others are born with natural talents and skills that emerge during their life. Often, in education, we miss out on finding each pupil's unique stamp because of the pressures of meeting targets, producing data, passing exams and then being accountable if we don't get it right. But as well as teaching a curriculum and supporting pupils to learn it, we need to try to unearth these skills and talents so they can be used to support and enhance the way our students learn and develop – the unveiling of the invisible stamp that tadcu told me about.

Have you ever wondered why some children easily manage a complex life including friends, schoolwork, and sports, while others drift through their school years confused and scattered? Or why two children can enter a maths class with equivalent ability and end the term with grades at opposite ends of the spectrum? To make the most of what we are born with, we need the skills of self-understanding and decision-making – that is, knowing who you are and then making choices that will be just right for you.

Dr Sidney Moon's description of personal talent as the 'exceptional ability to select difficult goals that fit with your interests, abilities, values, and contexts' helps to explain this puzzling phenomena.[1] Individuals with personal talent need to know themselves well, to be helped to make good decisions and then to combine this with the skills needed to accomplish their goals. They are also resilient and self-disciplined individuals with high levels of context-specific personal talent, which allows them to balance multiple, competing and challenging goals, such as working in a demanding profession as well as being part of a family and having external hobbies and interests. What we need to do as educators is to find each child's talents and slowly, during their learning life, help them to develop the skills that will reveal their invisible stamp.

---

1 Sidney Moon, Extraordinary Lives and Difficult Goals, *Center for Talent Development, School of Education and Social Policy, Northwestern University* (n.d.). Available at: http://www.ctd.northwestern.edu/resources/displayArticle/?id=141/.

In order to exploit their personal talent, an individual needs to combine self-knowledge with an awareness of the environment within which they operate. Self-knowledge is all about recognising your personal interests, abilities and skills as well as your life and learning values. Knowing your environment enables you to work out how to accomplish certain goals within that environment, as well as understanding what factors may stop you from succeeding. Effectively, these are self-analytical tools. For example, some learners need to be made aware of the ways that socio-economic and cultural conditions may inhibit their personal aspirations and choices. For all of us, it is a process of learning through experience and testing our personal approaches in a variety of different situations. To what extent does your classroom give your children the opportunity to do this?

This is what good teachers do – we get our pupils to try different types of learning experiences so they can determine what works for them and what doesn't. And if the learner is unsure what is best because, for example, they don't have the social skills to extract this information, then it is our job as teachers to guide them.

Quite simply, it's about discovering what makes each child sparkle – their 'Ready Brek glow' (for those of you who remember the advertisement!) or what they are passionate about – which can then filter into their overall personal development and an enhanced approach to learning in the classroom. Watching, discovering and slowly unveiling the invisible stamp in the early years is the foundation to helping our children grow into healthy, well-rounded individuals. It's just another form of formative assessment, and from the assessment comes a deduction about the appropriate methods and strategies for learning which will suit the needs of each child.

When considering how to find each pupil's gifts and talents, **THINK** about:

- What do you know about each child?
- What are their family circumstances?
- Are they loved?
- What makes them happy?
- What makes them unhappy?
- How do they interact with their peers?
- How they respond to adults?
- Do they prefer learning and playing indoors or outdoors?

- Do they enjoy playing on their own?
- Do they enjoy playing with others?
- Are they curious about new things?
- Are they curious about how things work?
- Do they prefer books to toys?
- Do they enjoy singing and dancing?
- Do they enjoy making and creating?
- Are they confident?
- Are they withdrawn or disengaged during certain activities or tasks?
- Do they listen well to stories?
- Do they listen well to instructions?
- Do they demonstrate a curiosity about the world?
- Do they have some understanding of what is acceptable and what is unacceptable?
- Is there one particular thing they excel at?
- Can they solve simple problems?
- Are they able to create and ask questions?
- Do they feel safe?
- Are they able to distinguish between different emotions?

When it comes to finding a child's gifts and talents, use the following methods to collect information and then apply your observations to support their personal development and ignite their passion. This is how you will light the fire in their bellies.

 TRY this:

- Look at ways where you can *observe* them in order to *assess* them.
- So you can *analyse* your observations (maybe with colleagues).
- To come to *conclusions* about what best to do in the classroom.
- Which you then *evaluate* to see what really works for them.

- In order to *set learning and personal targets*.
- Which, in turn, leads to *differentiation* for inclusive learning in order to find each child's *invisible stamp*.

 On page 160 is a **RESOURCE** for your classroom. Can you help your students find their invisible stamp?

 Here's a **RESOURCE** you might find useful: http://www.wiltshire.gov.uk/eyfs-planning-examples-pack.pdf. Use the provision plan table on page 11 of this document to give your learners opportunities for personal growth and differentiated learning spaces that will help them to find their invisible stamps.

Let me know how it goes.

Resource from *Of Teaching, Learning and Sherbet Lemons* © Nina Jackson, Paul Wrangles, 2

25

SOUND WAVES *DO* MAKE BRAIN WAVES

Q I ONCE READ THAT MUSIC CAN HELP WITH LEARNING IN THE CLASSROOM. WHAT DO YOU THINK? WHAT MUSIC WORKS? HOW AND WHEN? WHAT ABOUT LETTING THEM LISTEN USING HEADPHONES?

A Following years of research on the effects of music on the learning brain, this is an area I feel that I can really help you with. And there is plenty of research on, and recommendations for, using the right music at the right time and for the right reasons in all sorts of learning and teaching situations. Using music specifically dedicated to learning is an area that seems to cause controversy with teachers. However, numerous studies have shown that using techniques linked with the theory of 'sound waves make brain waves' has helped learners with the way they approach learning.[1]

Music has the neural firepower to jazz up thought processes and reasoning skills. Listening to music can help learners encode information and improve the recall process. Getting the brain ready to recall information, solve problems, learn by rote, develop study and revision skills and even deduce theorems is a complex process. However, I've found that using music for focus can help learners and teachers with abstract reasoning and brainwork, such as analytical, creative or administrative thinking and aspects of motivation.[2] Using the right music can cut out distractions and structure thoughts for academic learning.

---

1 You can find the data to support this research in Ian Gilbert's *The Big Book of Independent Thinking: Do Things No One Does or Do Things Everyone Does In a Way No One Does* (Carmarthen: Crown House Publishing, 2006), p. 31.

2 See Jackson, *The Little Book of Music for the Classroom*, p. 7.

Music can also help students to work smarter, not harder. The accelerated learning school pioneered by Bulgarian psychologist Georgi Lozanov during the 1950s and 1960s, and then popularised in the United States by Sheila Ostrander and Lynn Schroeder, suggest that learning in time to music at about 60 beats per minute (BPM) helps imprint material in the memory with less conscious effort.[3] Learning to music is certainly an improvement on the usual grinding process of silent memorisation, so why shouldn't something that sounds good make the memory work better?

Certain kinds of music induce a receptive mood that generally enhances cognitive processing. Music can also serve as a memory aid to help students encode information, which in turn supports learning, recall and transference into working memory. (If I say 'Happy Birthday to you ...' your memory will take it from there, won't it!)

Music primes the mind for learning, whether you are deducing mathematical theorems, drawing conclusions from experiments, playing chess or being challenged by any type of abstract thinking. By using music correctly in the classroom, you will be able to stimulate aspects of the 'left brain' (yes, I know it's more complicated than that, hence the scare quotes!) in order to promote logical and analytical thinking, as well as stimulating 'right brain' (ditto!) thinking to help your students grasp the big picture and think in a non-verbal and creative way. Music also helps when they are studying for a test or examination or when they need to recall knowledge, information, shapes or pictures. In fact, by following my guidelines you will be able to develop the students' skills and processes to recall almost anything.

 THINK about this: by linking a piece of music or a melody to a fact, the pupils can make an instant link between the information they have been studying and the music they have heard. It acts as a 'brain trigger', much like storing information in a special little box. Playing the music is like opening the box. Easy really!

 Now **TRY** this technique with the pupils:

1. Explain to the pupils that you are going to assist them with memory recall. Present the information you want them to learn or memorise on a hand-out, worksheet or digital device.

---

3   Shelia Ostrander, Lynn Schroeder and Nancy Ostrander, *Super Learning 2000* (New York: Delacorte Press, 1994).

2. Tell the pupils that when the music starts they should listen to it with their eyes closed and follow the 'shape' of the melody. They can put their heads on the desk if that helps them to feel safe when their eyes are closed.

3. Play the music for a few minutes – a minimum of two but no more than ten. The pupils must *not* write down anything at this point. They should just listen to the music and become engrossed in it. This will link the music to their learning later on.

4. When you've finished playing the musical extract, ask the pupils to choose a suitable way of remembering the information. They may use jotting, noting, drawing, bullets, learning diary, doodling, mind maps or any other preferred form of note-taking as long it's a way of visualising what they have been thinking.

5. Play the same piece of music again for the same amount of time. This time tell the pupils to read the hand-out and link what they've learned to the shape of the melody. The brain will now begin to make a link between the learning and the music.

6. Towards the end of the lesson, play the music one more time (with the volume level low) and get the pupils to show or tell you what they can remember, either in groups or as individuals. You will soon see how the music has linked with the facts to enhance memory recall.

7. Check to see if this has worked in the following lesson by playing the same piece of music again and assessing how much they can recall. When the music begins to trigger a link in the brain, they should remember doing the task or recall specific learning patterns. Don't leave it too long before repeating the exercise as their memories may begin to fade.

 On page 164 is a **RESOURCE** you can use to inspire you to use music in your classroom.

Resource from *Of Teaching, Learning and Sherbet Lemons* © Nina Jackson, Paul Wrangles, 2C

Here is a list of musical **RESOURCES** you could think about using. These extracts have been chosen because they are between 80–120 BPM. Research suggests that timbres, textures and frequencies at this tempo support memory recall because sound pulses create alpha waves associated with concentration and meditative states.

MOZART MUSICAL EXTRACTS

- Adagio in E for Violin and Orchestra
- Clarinet Concerto in A Major: Adagio
- Divertimento No. 2: Adagio
- Divertimento No. 11: Molto allegro (in D major)
- Divertimento No. 15: Adagio
- Flute and Harp Concerto: Andantino
- Flute Quartet No. 1: Adagio
- Piano Concerto No. 21: Andante
- Piano Concerto No. 23: Adagio
- Serenade No. 10 ('Gran Partita'): Adagio
- Serenade No. 13 for Strings (*Eine kleine Nachtmusik*): Allegro and Romanze
- String Quartet No. 20 in D Major K.499 (*Hoffmeister*): Adagio I and III
- String Quartet No. 21: Andante
- Symphony No. 35: 3rd movement
- Violin Concerto No. 3: Adagio

It's not just about Mozart, you know, so here are some other suggestions:

- Adolph Adam – *Giselle*: 'Valse'
- Geoffrey Burgon – soundtrack from *Brideshead Revisited*: 'The Hunt', 'Sebastian Against the World' and 'Julia'
- Fauré – Pavane (modern version from *Utopia*, 2001)

- Jean Michel Jarre – *Oxygene*
- Robert Prizeman – *Libera*: 'Mysterium'
- Schubert – *Rosamunde*
- Vivaldi – Flute Concerto No. 3 in D Major: Allegro
- Vivaldi – Concerto for 2 Trumpets in C Major
- Liquid – 'Sweet Harmony' (original mix)

If you would like to know more about the specific aspects of using music for learning then please do jot me a line and I will get back to you. That's what the Ninja does – always happy to help!

Now, what about the prickly notion of children using headphones in class to listen to music? Well, once you have educated the pupils about choosing the right type of music for the right reasons when they are working, they will be able to choose appropriate extracts linked with that type of work or task. Headphones enable the children to become more engrossed in their work as they are not distracted by other sounds in the classroom. Please make sure you advise your students not to listen to music with lyrics if they are involved in any type of written task, as this will cause what is known as a 'dual-task paradigm' in the brain. This means the words they are thinking and the words they are listening to come into conflict. (Imagine if a bit of Eminem emerged in the written work of one of your pupils – mind you, it might spice up your marking for the week!)

 THINK about this: do you ever find yourself struggling to get your learners to be calm (especially if you feel as if you're ready to explode)? If so, music can help. Aristotle referred to music as medicine because of its calming and cathartic powers. This is something you can utilise in your classroom to help students deal with unwanted emotions. And it works for you too! Try using music to vent and channel your anger, frustration and grief, as well as the anger, frustration and poor behaviour of your class.

A tremendous amount of evidence has been collated about the connection between hardcore music styles and aggressive or violent behaviour. Some research has suggested that music, such as heavy metal, rock and hardcore rap, leads to aggression, violence and activities like drug abuse. Other findings suggest that exposure to violent media images correlates with behaviour and attitude problems, particularly among adolescent males. However, none of these investigations has conclusively proved that listening to hardcore music leads to aggressive or self-destructive behaviour. It seems more likely that angry, at risk young people have a preference for 'negative' music, which they use not as a healthy catharsis but as an affirmation of their troubled state. Furthermore, many controlled studies that link music to an undesirable effect or behaviour have supplemented the music with strong visual images. These results don't describe the effect music has on people, but rather testify to the way music has been appended to television, movie and video images to heighten the emotional experience.

While such debate is important, it often overlooks the fact that intense music has been composed for thousands of years across the world. Listening to a variety of the 'right' music – from Beethoven's Fifth Symphony to the explosive vocalising of Kecak music from Bali – will not cause you any issues with aggression or violence. It is more useful to reflect that people throughout time have made music to serve vital personal and social purposes. For example, the lyrical message of some rap music is very powerful, but it is only when the frequencies and tones of the instruments are incoherent to the musical ear that it becomes an issue.

Most of the pupils in your classroom will at some point display anger, frustration or grief. The message here is to make sure you do not increase the intensity of these behaviours by shouting or raising your own voice in order to get the students on task. Instead, use appropriate music to calm down groups and individuals and help them to achieve a more focused, forward-thinking state of mind.

And headphones have a big part to play. I advocate the use of personal headphones for anyone who displays behaviour that is affecting not only their own work but also that of others. If the majority of the class is focused and ready for learning, then you can ask those who are not ready to remove themselves into a quiet personal zone of music. They can do this when they realise – or you tell them – that their behaviour is out of control. The combination of the right music and headphones with a student who has withdrawn from the main learning group will help them to regulate their behaviour and allow them to become more focused on the tasks and learning ahead. This is *not* a reward. This is using music as a tool to support learning. Try it!

It would be a good idea to use these musical extracts as your **RESOURCE** for supporting learning with headphones:

- Samuel Barber – Adagio for Strings
- Ennio Morricone – soundtrack from *The Mission*: 'On Earth As It Is In Heaven' and 'Gabriel's Oboe'
- Michael Nyman – soundtrack from *The Piano*: 'The Heart Asks Pleasure First'
- Karl Jenkins – *Adiemus Live*: 'Adiemus' and 'The Wooing of Etain'
- Hans Zimmer – soundtrack from *Gladiator*: 'Now We Are Free'
- Anastasi – *CinemOcean*
- Enya – *Paint the Sky with Stars*
- Steven Halpern – *Serenity Suite: Music and Nature Sounds*
- Hisham – *Somewhere in a Dream*
- Georgia Kelly – *Seapeace*
- Kitaro – *Mandala*
- Ray Lynch – *Deep Breakfast*
- Harry Pickens – *Peace & Quiet*
- Paul Winter – *Common Ground*
- Yanni – *Devotion (The Best of Yanni)*
- Libera – 'Salva Me', 'Sanctus' and 'Agnus Dei'
- Craig Leon and Izzy – 'Libera Me'

Good luck, and do let me know how you get on.

26
SELF-HARM

Q THERE IS A GIRL IN MY CLASS WHO I BELIEVE IS SELF-HARMING. WHAT SHOULD I DO?

A Many teachers and young people are unwilling to address the taboo subject of self-harm. However, self-harming is on the rise among young people, particularly during examination time.[1] And there have been horrifying cases of children as young as 5 self-harming by cutting and burning themselves, drinking toxic chemicals and taking overdoses.[2] According to Child Line, the number of boys self-harming has risen by 30%, and these are only the reported cases. In some parts of the UK it has reached an 'epidemic level' according to Chris Leaman of the Young Minds charity.[3] Statistics show than one in every 12 children self-harm in the UK.[4] So, self-harm is a growing concern which must be addressed in schools, communities and families.

Self-harming involves an individual intentionally choosing to damage their body. For some, it's a way of coping with distress, trauma and difficult emotions, such as self-esteem issues, the pressure of school and examinations and problems at home. It is a form of self-punishment and can address the need in some young people to 'feel alive' in the face of what they perceive as a lack of ability to feel anything at all.

---

1 The Telegraph, GCSEs: Pressure of Exams Leaves Teens Suffering from Mental Illness (25 August 2011). Available at: http://www.telegraph.co.uk/education/educationnews/8720513/GCSEs-Pressure-of-exams-leaves-teens-suffering-from-mental-illness.html/.

2 Amelia Hill, Even 5-Year-Olds Are At Risk from Self-Harm, Parents Are Warned, *The Guardian* (3 August 2008). Available at: http://www.theguardian.com/society/2008/aug/03/mentalhealth.children/.

3 Anna Edwards, 'Epidemic' of Children As Young As Five Self-Harming Warns Charity, *Daily Mail* (5 February 2013). Available at: http://www.dailymail.co.uk/news/article-2273638/Epidemic-children-young-self-harming-warns-charity.html/.

4 Sarah Boseley, Self-Harm Practised By One In 12 Adolescents, Study Reveals, *The Guardian* (17 November 2011). Available at: http://www.theguardian.com/society/2011/nov/17/self-harm-in-adolescents-study/.

Self-harm is any type of self-destructive behaviour, such as self-cutting, swallowing objects, burning with lighters or cigarettes, running in front of cars, pinching until they bruise, throwing themselves down the stairs, taking steroids or unsuitable protein shakes and purposefully adopting eating disorders. The important factor is that the act is deliberate. Self-harming can become addictive to some young people and should therefore be taken very seriously.

Young people have reported that the reason they self-harm is to:

● Vent anger and frustration.

● Gain control.

● Numb themselves from the outside world.

● Stop bad thoughts and emotions.

● Release tension.

● Comfort themselves so that they are in control and not anybody else.

● See 'red' – the blood (if cutting) gives them the reality that they are alive.

● Punish themselves for not being good enough for their parents, teachers or their own expectations.

● To take away the numbness and check they are able to feel pain and shame.

● Replace emotional pain with physical pain.

● Have an adrenaline rush.

There are different levels of self-harm. In extreme cases, some will choose self-harm because they want to die, but more often than not it's about expressing distress or relieving feelings of unbearable tension, unhappiness and stress. At times, self-harm can be a cry for help. Some individuals will show others what they have done in order to ask for help, but others will not. It's a complex emotional illness, but with the right care, support and counselling, the individual can stop.

Some self-harm is severe and will need medical support and treatment, but other young people can be helped through it by the school, their family, the community and even online help.

THINK about these risk factors which are linked with self-harming:

- Low mood (or feeling down).
- Anxiety and stress (particularly during examinations).
- Psychological or developmental difficulty, such as a learning difference, Asperger's, ADD or ADHD.
- Difficulty in communication or sharing thoughts with others.
- Low self-esteem.
- Difficulty with solving personal problems and issues at school or home.
- Hopelessness.
- Drug or alcohol abuse.
- Confusion about sexuality or feeling different/unaccepted.
- Bullying and lack of friends or a supportive friendship group.
- Unreasonable expectations at home.
- Trauma, domestic violence and abuse.
- Cultural identity dilemmas and conflict linked to religion and ethnicity.
- Poor parental relationships leading to arguments and conflict.
- Depression or mental illness in the family.
- Young people acting as carers.
- Racism and homophobia.

There could be a number of factors that might have changed in your student's life and some of these might help you to approach the subject with her. If you believe she is self-harming, ask yourself whether you have seen changes involving any of the following possible triggers:

- Mood, activity and participation in class.
- Eating habits.
- Increased isolation from peer groups and family.
- Changes in academic results.
- Talking about self-harming and/or suicide.

- Other pupils showing concern.
- Becoming irritable or aggressive.
- Becoming socially withdrawn at school and at home.
- Drug or alcohol abuse.
- Giving away personal possessions.
- Expressing feelings of failure or never being 'good enough'.
- Feeling that they can never reach their own expectations, especially if they are gifted and talented pupils.

Once self-harm has started (especially cutting) it's very difficult for some young people to stop. When a young person inflicts pain on themselves, the body will respond by releasing endorphins, a natural pain reliever that can give temporary relief to an upsetting situation and a sense of overall peace and well-being. The compulsion can make it hard for the individual to stop as the adrenaline rush from the pain is momentarily quite wonderful. In other words, it becomes addictive.

THINK about this visualisation of self-harming:

SELF-HARM

Negative emotions
(anger, despair, sadness)

The tension phase
(unable to control emotions, dissociation due to coping with tension)

The act of self-harm
(burning, cutting, etc.)

The feel-good factor
(negative feelings gone for a short time, endorphins released)

Feeling bad
(shame, pain, infection from cuts, guilt)

 TRY these suggestions to help your pupil:

- Ask the pupil if they would like to have a chat with you, or just a catch-up, on how things are in general in order to ease any concerns you may have.
- If, after your chat, you believe the pupil is self-harming, make sure you tell the young person that although you will be very supportive, she must understand the limits of your confidentiality – that it will be your duty to report it to the right people who can help and will not judge her. This is very important as you could inadvertently spark further self-harming during this time.

- Do not judge the pupil at any point. Even saying, 'Oh, that's awful,' could create a tipping point. Reassure the pupil that you understand the self-harm is helping her to cope at the moment, but that you are the main support link here.

- Offer information about support agencies (but remember that some internet sites may contain inappropriate information and users). There are some great groups on Twitter, such as YoungMinds (@YoungMindsUK), Mental Health Ed (@MentalHealth_Ed), the Blurt Foundation (@BlurtAlerts), Mental Health Foundation (@MHF_tweets) and MindFull (@MindFullUK). You might also want to mention using #MentalHealth, but please make sure you reassure the pupil that she is not 'mental'!

- Just being there can be a support tool in itself. What is very important for young people is knowing there is someone there for them to talk to – someone who will listen, properly, and will not judge them in any way. It could be you, a school counsellor, nurse, head of year or pastoral worker – anyone who can really listen. A self-harmer will usually seek out someone who makes them feel 'safe'.

- Control contagion. Be vigilant in case close friends of the pupil are also self-harming. Each individual may have different reasons for self-harming and should be given the opportunity for one-to-one support. It may also be helpful to discuss the matter openly if a group of young people is involved.

- Support of peers. The individual may want to pass information to you via a peer or group of friends. Generally, friends will tell you anyway if they are concerned about another individual.

You may also want to introduce the young person to some self-coping strategies, such as:

- Having 'quiet time' during school – a safe place to go.
- Keeping a diary.
- Listening to music, but the right music (you can find information about this in my book, *The Little Book of Music for the Classroom*).
- Writing, drawing and talking about their feelings.
- Looking after a pet.
- Drawing red lines on the skin instead of cutting, then washing them away and seeing how clean the skin is.

- Clenching ice cubes in the hand until they melt away – this can relieve tension.
- Using the Rainbow Journal.[5]

I see this as more about developing good emotional and mental health as a daily regime for prevention rather than dealing with a medically diagnosed issue, although it can lead to this if the right support is not offered. When we consider the increase in mental and emotional health problems in our schools, it's time we all pulled together and stopped the shame and discomfort with talking about or addressing mental health issues, for the sake of our pupils and our staff. Together, we need to make young people more aware of the support on offer and the safety net available in each school.

I would advocate that you work with your head teacher to devise and create the following:

- A school policy on mental and emotional health issues and an agreed confidentiality approach.
- A list of crisis telephone numbers aimed at pupils and staff to be displayed around the school along with useful Twitter links.
- Greater openness – educate the whole school and make mental health a topic of discussion every day, much like the weather.
- A school safety plan of support for all.
- A policy of sharing – encourage pupils and colleagues to be 'good friends' by communicating any concerns about a person in distress or who exhibits a change of personality.

This is an area that is close to my heart, so if you would like me to come to your school to support you with this, then please get in touch. I have worked with many teachers, parents and children on mental and emotional health issues and strategies for coping and helping. This will give you the opportunity to find out about the 'Whisperers and the Listeners' approach I have developed, which will be of benefit to your pupils, staff, parents and governors.

On page 176 is a **RESOURCE** you can use in your classroom to reassure any students who you think may be at risk.

---

5   For more information see: www.selfinjurysupport.org.uk/self-injury-self-help-ideas/.

Resource from *Of Teaching, Learning and Sherbet Lemons* © Nina Jackson, Paul Wrangles, 20

Here are some great **RESOURCES** – well-researched and supportive websites:

- The Blurt Foundation

  www.blurtitout.org

  @BlurtAlerts

- YoungMinds

  www.youngminds.org.uk

  Parent helpline: 0808 802 5544

- Samaritans

  www.samaritans.org

  24 hour helpline: 08457 90 90 90

- ChildLine

  www.childline.org.uk

  24 hour helpline: 0800 1111

- CALM (Campaign Against Living Miserably)

  www.thecalmzone.net

  Helpline for men (5 p.m. to 12 a.m.): 0800 58 58 58

- PAPYRUS (Prevention of Young Suicide)

  www.papyrus-uk.org

  Helpline (Monday to Friday: 10 a.m. to 10 p.m., weekends/bank holidays: 2 p.m. to 5 p.m.): 0870 170 4000

- TESS

  Text/email support for girls and young women up to 25 who self-injure

  Open Monday to Friday: 7 p.m. to 9 p.m.

  Text number: 0780 047 2908

  Email accessed via: www.selfinjury.org.uk

- National Self-Harm Network

  www.nshn.co.uk

- SANE

  www.sane.org.uk

  Helpline (6 p.m. to 11 p.m.): 0845 767 8000

- Mind

  www.mind.org.uk

- Time to Change

  www.time-to-change.org.uk

- Centre for Mental Health

  www.centreformentalhealth.org.uk/info/mental_health_information.aspx

One in four of us will suffer a mental health issue during our lifetime, so it's time for us all to change the stigma and taboo around mental and emotional health and illness. We are all in this together.

Good luck, and please keep in touch and let me know how things go.

27

HOW WILL I KNOW?

Q I'VE BEEN ASKED TO APPLY FOR A MANAGEMENT POST IN MY SCHOOL, BUT I'M NOT SURE IF I'M LEADERSHIP MATERIAL. HOW WILL I KNOW?

A Congratulations on being spotted as someone who may be able to lead and manage learning and teaching in your school! When we are classroom teachers, we sometimes forget that we are natural leaders and managers in our own right. When it comes to discovery, questioning, exploration and growth, we manage the learning, the teaching, the pupils, ourselves and we lead others to pastures new. But when we talk about management and leadership in schools, many teachers are put off by the idea of working with teams of people and making difficult decisions which some might not agree with. So, I would like to mention a colleague, and a friend, who is an outstanding leader, a brilliant head teacher, who makes difficult decisions on a daily basis, has a class of hundreds of children and manages hundreds of staff.

Welcome to the world of Vic Goddard, head teacher at Passmores Academy, star of *Educating Essex* (although he won't thank me for that, I'm sure!) and someone who believes that being a head teacher is, as he describes in the title of his book, 'the best job in the world'.[1] For Vic, leading, managing and working in education is an amazing privilege, and here I must say I wholeheartedly agree. There is nothing better than seeing young people grow into adults ready to hit the real world when they leave our schools and become future makers, community creators and worldwide impactors.

Your current role in the classroom has a massive impact on your pupils, but so too would your role as a leader and manager. Bigger maybe! If you are concerned about not being in the classroom as much, then negotiate your role so that this still includes

---

1 Vic Goddard, *The Best Job in the World* (Carmarthen: Independent Thinking Press, 2014).

teaching time. You will have much more respect from your colleagues if you continue in this vein. We often lose amazing teachers to management positions, but it is worth remembering that outstanding teachers do not always make great managers, and great managers have not always been outstanding teachers. We all have our gifts and talents and they manifest themselves in different ways.

If you have never thought about being a manager or leader and you are surprised you have been asked to apply for a leadership job, you might want to ask your colleague what they see in you that makes them think you will be great at the job. We often don't see what others see in us, and can be blinded by our personal thoughts of what we are good at and, most often, not good at. Our perceptions of ourselves can be masked by what we think we are like, rather than how others actually view us. We are very good at judging ourselves! So, go ahead and ask away. It's a good learning curve. Honesty and truth can be make or break, but being a reflective practitioner will allow you to evaluate frankly what others see in you.

 THINK about this: to be really sure if something is right for you often means you have to experience it. Only then will you know if it works for you or if it doesn't. You may want to ask whether you could take on a role on a temporary basis to see if it's for you, on the understanding that if it isn't you can move back into the position you have previously loved. Alternatively, you may want to shadow a manager for a while to see if it is something you want to explore further. It will give you a great insight into what a leadership role would entail.

Being a manager is a process. It requires strength, experience, learning and practice. That's what we teachers do on a daily basis, but being in a management position means that you will need to work with, lead, support and develop teams of people too. Do you feel this is something you could do? If so, are you sure you want to?

 TRY thinking about these statements and see whether or not you are happy with the answers:

- I have the ability and compassion to influence others in their work so that progress can be made.
- I am confident in my abilities to positively influence an outstanding learning culture in the school.
- I can create a model for building a credible strategic plan within the school.
- I have ideas and can develop a process for creating measurable goals.

- I believe I have a good understanding of how and when to effectively delegate.

- I have the ability to break down complex functions into measurable tasks and be able to assess their impact.

- I believe I can build collaborative working teams within the school.

- I am confident in facilitating career development plans and supporting others, as well as myself, with CPD.

- I feel I have the necessary skills to address conflict resolution.

- I have the skills to structure, facilitate and lead difficult conversations with colleagues.

- I believe I could manage my personal stress with support.

- As a manager I would use best practice in delivering performance reviews.

- I could confidently chair and run a meeting.

- I have the skills to understand the role of critical thinking in management.

- I have good people skills and would be able to be empathetic as well as professional.

- I would put the heart of my teachers and learners at the forefront.

If you are able to think positively about at least half of the above, then I would suggest you do consider yourself for the post. Nobody is a born leader or manager, and often we learn from working with others and taking on intermediary roles.

It would be good for you to have an honest and frank discussion with your own line manager and ask them to give you an appraisal that covers why you would be suitable for the post. Also, consider in what areas you would like preliminary support and guidance. Sometimes individuals get appointed to a position because they are willing to learn – experience doesn't always count. Your inner passion, drive and determination to do a good job can win over an interview panel over. Oh yes, and your own self-belief!

 On page 182 is a **RESOURCE** which may help you.

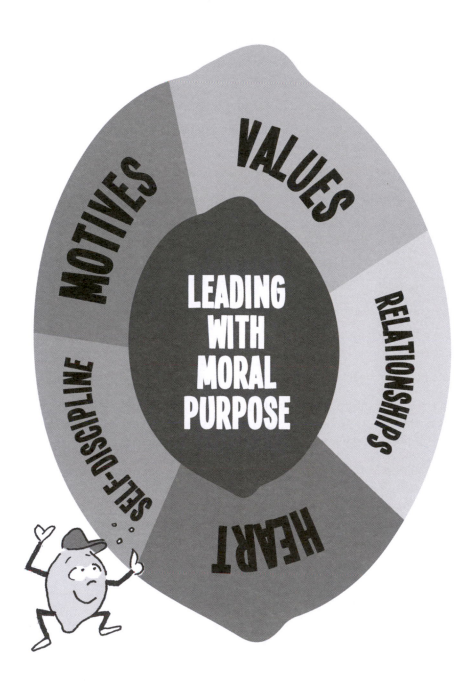

Resource from *Of Teaching, Learning and Sherbet Lemons* © Nina Jackson, Paul Wrangles, 2C

Here's another **RESOURCE** for you to use: *Leadership with a Moral Purpose: Turning Your School Inside Out* by Will Ryan (Carmarthen: Crown House Publishing, 2008). You cannot lift it off the page. You cannot truly see what is inside. But what it contains is an amazing analysis of turning leadership inside out. I believe this would be an excellent resource for you to explore as part of your own leadership dilemma.

28

TIPS FOR TRANSITION

Q I THINK TRANSITION FROM MY PRIMARY SCHOOL TO THE LOCAL SECONDARY SCHOOL COULD BE SO MUCH BETTER. WHAT CAN I DO ABOUT IT?

A Transition can be a very daunting experience for many young people. If pupils have siblings at the senior school then that can help, but many children are troubled by the myths and legends that surround the 'big school', which can make it seem a terrifying place, especially when viewed from the safety of their primary school.

All good transition ensures there is a healthy emotional and academic link between the feeder primary schools and local secondary schools, whether that's a comprehensive, a flash new academy or a free school. Wherever they end up, the overarching rule of effective relationships should remain the same: the new children should feel safe, happy and able to ask for help.

Teaching and learning is a continuous part of life for all children in the education system, but transitional learning is an area which as a profession we really need to develop further. Let me ask you a question: should the preparation for the move from primary to secondary school begin in Year 6? I'm not sure what you think, but my response is quite definitely no – it should begin much sooner!

Here are some ideas for you to **THINK** about:

● Cross-phase teaching and learning between primary and secondary schools is an excellent way of sharing teaching and learning ideas, communicating thinking and improving educational networking. The more primary pupils from can gain experiences of working alongside older children and a group of different teachers, the more adept and prepared they will be for the physical move.

- Schools that collaborate on topics or projects of interest can share learning with one another at special cross-phase community events. These might include working with bridging materials, social events, music/drama evenings, pupil workshops and taster days/evenings from Year 4 upwards.

- 'Getting to know you' activities or community festivals can generate a plethora of interesting, fun and active sessions. I've visited schools in Chile which have spectacular family days. They are open to parents, aunties, grandparents and anybody from the community, who can all join in the most outrageously hysterical group activities ever experienced. In one school, I witnessed a grandmother of 85 doing Zumba, and she was better than I was (not surprising, really, if you knew my special shape and size)! But the best thing was that *everyone* was laughing, joking, getting involved and generally having one great day of being together, which could only have positive future benefits for the schools and communities involved.

- I would like to see every pupil making the transition from primary to secondary presented with a map of the school on a t-shirt. During the first couple of weeks, the t-shirt would form part of the uniform, and all pupils in the secondary school would wear them too. I think even the teachers and most definitely the head teacher should too. Wouldn't this be a total community approach to supporting newcomers and helping them to get around?

- Don't forget the toilets! These are so important for new pupils. I often think that flashing disco lights around the toilets wouldn't go amiss in some schools. At least it would put a buzz into the new academic year and give all pupils something to talk about apart from 'Who have you got for maths?' or how quickly they can graffiti their books. Before you think I've completely lost the plot with this one, it isn't a joke or one of my crazy Ninja ideas. I once mentioned it to a secondary school and they went ahead and put flashing disco lights around the toilet entrances and even had balloons in the dinner hall! Why would you worry about joining a new school when you could think of it as being a party every day. Bring it on, I say!

- I'm a keen advocate of buddies, mates, learning groupies or just plain minders (in the caring sense of the word). Call them what you like, but sometimes wearing a badge or highlighting that the older children are there to help and look after the younger ones really does go a long way. (I wish I'd had a buddy when I joined secondary school, as I spent most of my time crying because I had to wear these stupid size 8 flat black shoes, because they were 'sensible', only to discover when I got there that most of my friends had really trendy ones.)

- Put information booklets to good use, preferably produced as a digital resource as well as a printed version. These are always given the thumbs-up by parents and children. Digital books can be emailed to parents and you will save a fortune on your school's postal charges.

- Get the stationery right. It's always a good idea to tell parents what the basic stationery toolkit should contain because, for most children, the right tools for the job can make or break a lesson or learning experience. Secondary school should also have 'emergency packs' or cool pencil cases and the like for the most vulnerable and disadvantaged young people. Make contact with the feeder primary schools so you can identify these students and help them to prepare. In my local area, a chapel contacts primary schools to find out who these children and families might be and then anonymously posts a package to the house with a note saying, 'We wish you luck in your new school, from all your friends in the community.' These packages contain pencil cases (very trendy ones), pens, pencils, rulers, etc. – the usual – and, most importantly for some young people, a lucky £1 coin which is in an envelope marked 'For emergencies – and that's NOT chocolate!' I know one young lad who is now 16 and still has the £1 coin. He once told me, 'It's for an emergency, and as yet I haven't had to use it!' So, who knows, this £1 may stay with him for a very long while yet!

- Make sure administrative records are in order. Effective and robust systems of pupil data and records for key school staff are essential. The best teachers really know the students they are teaching, and the sooner that can happen the better.

- Get parents on board and invite them to informal evenings to look around the school, experience different subject areas, meet the teachers and get to know the most crucial people (i.e. the reception and administration staff, as they will probably be the first point of contact for any parent or carer). Make sure parents know who the head of year or pastoral team leader is for their child. After all, a happy child is the most important thing in any learning environment.

- Moving on with most of their primary school friends can help with successfully building new relationships as the children will feel safe if their friends are close by. If they are not in the same class, make sure they know where they are and can find them during those crucial breaktimes and lunchtimes.

- Empower children to have an honest and open dialogue with their parents about the move. If a child feels they can't do this, ask them to create a 'worry and wisdom' box for their house, like a friend of mine did. The child could put a note in the box when the parents/carers weren't around and then the parent could address this over dinner or in an informal way – when out for an ice cream or a walk in the park. It doesn't have to be an official 'family meeting' as this could cause further upset and worry. Primary schools might want to install these boxes in their own schools, or be adventurous and call them 'things I'm thinking about' boxes or jars. Popping a secret note into a box is always a lovely thing to do, especially when no one is looking!

 You might like to **TRY** this technique and suggest it to the pupils, parents and staff in both schools. I call it the '3P perfection plan': plan, personalise, prepare = perfection.

3P PERFECTION PLAN

- **Plan.** Find out well in advance details about any specific learning or living differences a pupil has and involve the parents, pastoral teams and SENCO. Moving around a secondary school is much harder than a primary school, so any physical differences need to be taken into account. Also consider common medical needs, such as diabetes, asthma, etc. For example, we forget that some children find climbing stairs a serious physical strain.

- **Personalise.** Get the transition teams in the various schools to consider personalising the whole process of transition by meeting the individual needs of the pupils – learning, emotional *and* cultural. An example of this would be to create personalised learning planners. Get the Year 6 children to add to their planners everything they are confident and happy with in relation to their learning, hobbies, interests and concerns rather than spending copious amounts of time at the beginning of the new academic year copying timetables and school details into their planners. Make it relevant, real and personal.

- **Prepare.** In today's world of QR codes and augmented reality, create videos and digital links to help the students to find their way around. This would also be good CPD exercise for all staff in the school to become involved in a new way of learning and communication. I like to call it 'digilearning'. Talk to current students about their experiences of transition and learn from it. Also seek feedback from parents in Year 7 about their children's experience in the first term. Honesty is always the best policy, so be prepared!

 On page 190 is a **RESOURCE** you can use to help with the transition process.

PLAN, PERSONALISE & PREPARE...

TO ACHIEVE PERFECTION!

Resource from *Of Teaching, Learning and Sherbet Lemons* © Nina Jackson, Paul Wrangles, 20

29

THE SHAPE OF THE SPOON

Q I REALLY WANT TO GET MY CHILDREN TO THINK FOR THEMSELVES AND FIND OUT THINGS ON THEIR OWN, BUT THERE IS SO MUCH PRESSURE TO COVER THE SYLLABUS IN TIME FOR THE TEST. HOW DO I MAKE SURE THEY DO WELL IN THE TEST WITHOUT JUST SPOON FEEDING THEM?

A I am delighted I have a question from a teacher who wants to get children thinking for themselves, rather than regurgitating what a teacher once taught them or simply teaching pupils how to pass a test or exam. Hallelujah! As a wise man once said, 'If we're not teaching them to think then what are we teaching them?'

Even though we teachers are continuously under pressure to get our pupils to pass exams and achieve the best grades they can, because this reflects on the school's ranking in the league tables, this does not necessarily mean that children are learning how to think, how to unravel that thinking or how to produce their own ideas. It just means we are grooming them to pass exams. Lots of robots all doing the same thing and churning out the same information does not a human race make!

While there is a big element of teaching for and to the test in education, we really must get our students to break down the thinking behind what they are learning. Without this they may not be able to understand the 'whats' and the 'whys' hidden within the learning process. Questioning and thinking about the syllabus and the learning it contains can generate wonderful opportunities to dig deeper and really unpick the thinking and the learning about *what* is being taught. It can encourage young people to question what is behind the knowledge — what underpins the areas of study. This will lead them to an understanding of the place of that learning in the wider world — if it has one, of course! (I'm not sure that I've ever needed to use quadratic equations or Pythagoras's theorem in life beyond a maths exam, but I have questioned how Pythagoras came up with his theorem on many occasions. Isn't that a deep form of thinking that might inspire some of your children?)

Have you tried different types of thinking strategies and learning experiences in your classroom that could be linked to the syllabus? Maybe ask the students to create a short video of what they have learned, a podcast or a form of visualisation – an infograph, mind map or similar, especially if this is linked to a consolidation of the learning process. Instead of presenting the learning and thinking through text, deliver it and share it in different ways. After all, different learning experiences and opportunities are the foundation of inclusivity and differentiation.

 THINK about these questions:

- Do you ask the children to respond to the curriculum content by developing their own questions?
- Do the children have opportunities to share their thoughts with others about topics you cover or discuss?
- Can the children question you or others in the class about their own learning and thinking?
- Do the children have opportunities for DIRTy time (see Chapter 15)? This is time set aside to think about their thinking and learning.
- Do the children come and ask you 'Why' or 'What' or 'How'? If they do, then you *are* giving them thinking opportunities, but you can extend this by asking them to go off and discover answers for themselves.

It's all about giving the children opportunities to access different learning experiences, which is exactly what we should be doing as educationalists.

 When you are covering syllabus content, why don't you **TRY** these critical thinking questions on your learners:

COLLABORATION, COMMUNICATION, CREATIVITY AND REFLECTION

- What do you think about the learning content or what was said?

- In what ways could you share these questions?
- What is your thinking on the content or statements?
- What questions could you create about the content or discussion?
- How would you convince others that your thinking is the right thinking?
- What are the most creative ways you could share your thinking and make it accessible to others?
- How can you collaborate and communicate with others in your class to see what differences there are between your responses and theirs?
- Take some time to reflect on others' comments so you can think about learning from a different perspective.

PERSONAL REFLECTION

- How do you determine whether what you are thinking is true or not?
- Have you thought about alternative solutions to the problem?
- Can you explain why your thinking makes sense to you?
- What if it's not true?
- Can you express yourself using different language or explain yourself in a different way?

REASONING

- Why do you think your response works? Would it always, and why?
- How might you prove your thinking is the best response?
- Is your thinking really true?
- How would you argue against something, and can your mind be changed?

ANALYSIS

● How could you show and share differences and similarities?

● What thinking patterns do you have that could lead you to alternative answers?

● How many different possibilities can you think of?

● Would you always use the same type of thinking to analyse your responses, or would you be willing to listen to others?

LEARNING CONNECTIONS

● How does what you have learned link to daily occurrences and events?

● Which ideas make the most sense to you? Why?

● Are there any problems that feel familiar? Why?

● What kinds of examples have you thought of that could make this problem workable?

● What similar problems are linked with this issue?

When you use effective questioning to unravel children's learning, you might want to consider incorporating questions that also link to deep philosophical responses.

To help with this there's a **RESOURCE** on page 196 that you can put in your classroom.

Here's a **RESOURCE** of questions for you that might give them that 'Hmmm' moment, when they can develop thinking on a different level to curriculum thinking. These are questions you can adapt as part of the learning syllabus.

● What's worse – failing or never trying?

● What worries you most – doing things right or doing the right things?

● How old might you be if you didn't know how old you are?

● What powers would you need to change the world, and is power really essential to change things?

- If nobody judged you ever again would you do things differently or the same?
- Have you ever been with someone, said nothing and walked away feeling you've had the best conversation ever?
- How alive is being alive?
- Are you the type of friend you'd like to have as a friend?
- Why does love have two sides – the one that hurts so much and the one that is magical? Or does love not have any sides? Is it just perfection?
- What one piece of advice would you offer a new-born child?
- Would you break the law to save the one you love?
- If you push a lift button more than once do you think that makes it come faster?
- Who controls the life you lead? Is being led by others the right path to follow?
- Why do the things that make you happy not make others happy too?
- Why are you, you? What makes you, you and not the same as someone else?
- Are you really unique?
- What is normal? Who is normal? Is normal really normal?
- Why is it great not to be normal? Who made normal normal?
- Can you taste colours? What do they taste like?

You see – asking, or thinking, different questions can lead to some of the most intriguing and mind-bending experiences ever. If you can build these types of thinking questions into the curriculum and syllabus, then you will develop more independent learners and thinkers, which is what we all should be doing.

Resource from *Of Teaching, Learning and Sherbet Lemons* © Nina Jackson, Paul Wrangles, 201

30

ADD, ADHD, SOS!

Q MY QUESTION IS SIMPLE. I NEED HELP WITH MANAGING CHILDREN WHO HAVE ATTENTION DEFICIT DISORDER AND/OR ATTENTION DEFICIT HYPERACTIVITY DISORDER. I HAVE BEEN TEACHING FOR A NUMBER OF YEARS, BUT THIS IS THE FIRST TIME I HAVE HAD THREE IN ONE CLASS. I'M A LITTLE BEWILDERED, SO ANYTHING THAT CAN HELP ME TO HELP THESE CHILDREN WOULD BE APPRECIATED. WHAT CAN I DO?

A It seems as if more and more teachers are now being faced with new challenges in mixed ability classrooms. It's good to know that you want to help these young people to succeed and achieve, and I can see your obvious professionalism in wanting to support their learning.

I once asked a group of teachers the following question: which one of these children may have ADD/ADHD? (a) The hyperactive child who talks nonstop, can't sit still and is physically 'jittery', (b) the quiet dreamer who sits at her desk and stares off into space completely tuned away from everything and everybody, or (c) both (a) and (b). And the correct answer is ... (c).

There are three main characteristics of ADD/ADHD: inattention, hyperactivity and impulsivity. Which characteristics predominate makes all the difference between a diagnosis of ADD or ADHD. Children with ADD/ADHD may be:

- Inattentive. Not hyperactive or impulsive, but it almost seems as if they are in a daze at times.

- Hyperactive and impulsive. They are fully able to pay attention, even if they seem anxious or maybe slightly stressed.

● Inattentive, hyperactive and impulsive (the most common form of ADD/ADHD). These students will have 'episodes' of extreme behaviour and physical changes which can often be alarming for both teacher and child.

Children who only have the inattentive or daydreaming symptoms of ADD/ADHD sometimes become 'the invisible ones' as they do not display outbursts or different or challenging behaviours. As a result they can become quite withdrawn. However, inattentiveness does have consequences, such as getting into hot water with parents and teachers for not following directions or instructions, underperforming in school and clashing with other children over not playing by the rules.

When tasks are repetitive or boring, children with ADD/ADHD can quickly tune out (I know I would if tasks were boring, so maybe it's not the fault of the child but the teaching content!). It's not that they can't pay attention – when they are doing things they enjoy or hearing about topics they are interested in they have no trouble focusing and staying on task. So the teacher has to work on the 'tune in' theory, which means finding out what makes them tick.

Organising their daily school schedule and work commitments is harder for children with ADD/ADHD than it is for most children. Helping them to develop time management strategies is a good way of supporting them with their 'busy thinking' which is how it feels for many of them. Most of us need some kind of management system in our lives otherwise our own thinking and planning can go all over the place. It's like trying to think in the middle of a crowd of a million people with them all making a noise at the same time, rather than being able to think quietly or deeply on your own in a wide open space.

Keeping focused or on track is another common problem because they skip necessary steps and procedures as their brains are working overtime. Concentrating, thinking and unravelling what questions are being asked can be very tiring, especially if there are things going on around them. It is important, therefore, to make a quiet space or a thinking space for these children so they have the opportunity to gather their thoughts in a more methodical way.

 THINK about these indicators when working with ADD/ADHD children:

INATTENTIVENESS OR DAYDREAMING - ASSOCIATED WITH ADD

- They can often be careless – sometimes making mistakes but at other times just digressing off on to other things.
- They give the impression that they can't hear you when you are talking to them.
- Following instructions can be difficult – they need them in a more a prescriptive form like bullet points.
- Distraction is far more exciting than being focused.
- Finishing anything can be a challenge as they get bored easily. They like to have lots of interesting projects or tasks on the go simultaneously.
- The need for good planning tools is essential to help them with their lack of organisational skills.
- They lose things a lot!
- The finer details of things get missed or unheard.

HYPERACTIVITY, EXCESSIVE ENERGY OR PHYSICAL JITTERING - ASSOCIATED WITH ADHD

- Keeping still is not an option – it's all about go, go go. This could mean jumping, running or even climbing over objects, often at the most inappropriate times and in the most inappropriate spaces.
- They find it hard to be quiet for long periods of time and can be guilty of talking non-stop.
- Relaxation can be both a chore and a bore.
- They can unexpectedly leave their seats or working areas when everyone else is quiet or working.
- They may make odd sounds or noises that may be socially unacceptable in certain situations or ask inappropriate questions about the learning (although I used to do that a lot in boring lessons at school!).

- They have a short fuse and a quick temper, and occasionally can react to situations in an uncontrollable manner.

IMPULSIVITY – ASSOCIATED WITH ADD/ADHD

- They can interrupt conversations because they want to be the centre of attention.
- Waiting their turn in a game or line can be frustrating – they will want to do it there and then (or they feel they might explode).
- They make inappropriate comments at the wrong time, often blurting out what they are thinking without considering the consequences.
- They will guess at an answer rather than taking the time to solve a problem strategically.
- They find it difficult to listen to others and don't wait for the whole question to be presented.
- Their emotional intelligence is poor and they can be unaware in social situations.
- They can't keep their emotions to themselves – angry outbursts and temper tantrums are very common.

There are also many positive effects of living with ADD/ADHD, so it is important to think about the 'disorder' as simply another living and learning difference and not a disability. Living with ADD/ADHD has nothing to do with intelligence or talent. These children can often be artistically gifted and have as sound an intellect as the next person.

There are many great traits to be found in these children, so it is vital that you to tune into them in order to help them get their own thinking focused for learning. Once you do, you will see how the classroom can be a very rewarding experience, both for you as the teacher and for the ADD/ADHD learner. For example, they can be extremely flexible with their thinking – because they have to consider so many options at one time they can be very open to different ideas, so will often give you multiple answers or responses. Some teachers see this as a real gift and talent. I used to regard children with ADD/ADHD as 'hot thinkers' – the need to share their answers immediately was like a burning fire inside, so getting the response out in the open means they can cool down their thinking. Their enthusiasm and spontaneity means life with them is rarely boring, and they can have very lively, lovely and interesting personalities. They can also be extremely eloquent and great fun, but you do need to tap into and harness their high energy.

When they are motivated the energy and drive of ADD/ADHD children is magical. They can work hard, play equally hard and just want to succeed at everything – like most other children. However, they can take the competitive aspect of a task very seriously, and if they don't meet their own expectations they can often become extremely frustrated, sometimes angry and aggressive too. It can be very difficult to get them away from a task or activity which interests them, especially if it's an active one – you'll have to prise them away from it sometimes! The four-to-one positive/negative praise system will come in very handy with these children.

The creativity of a child with ADD/ADHD often has no boundaries, so they can engage in multiple thinking scenarios all at once, and their imagination is really wonderful. The child who daydreams and has ten different thoughts simultaneously can become a master problem-solver or an inventive artist. Children with ADD/ADHD may be easily distracted, but equally they notice what others don't see. And what others don't see can often be the spark for new ideas and thinking, which can work brilliantly in class or in group work. Being different – seeing and doing things differently – keeps us on our toes as teachers too!

 TRY my tried and tested tips and strategies for working with pupils who have ADD/ADHD:

- Make sure that any child who has ADD/ADHD has an EHCP which is reviewed by the school and the parents. Where possible, the pupil should have personal input into the plan. Essentially, you want to make sure you have the correct diagnosis, rather than the school labelling the child with ADD/ADHD when there has been no formal medical assessment. This will then give you information about the type of ADD/ADHD that you need to plan for.

- Accept the child for who they are – do not attempt to change or mould their personality or behaviour. Remember the Ninja mantra: we are all the same and yet we are all different!

- Develop positive, emotional and academic relationships with the parents/carers. They will really appreciate this. Sometimes parents use great strategies at home that can be applied in the classroom and vice versa. How about creating a 'celebration journal' that could be shared between home and school?

- Ask for help if you need it – speak up and do not just soldier on. That's not fair on either you or the child.

- Use the child as a resource and relationship model. Ask them: what lesson was the best they have ever been in? What was their worst ever lesson? How were the two lessons different? Try to unpack the child's learning preferences with their help.

- Does the child know why they are a little different? Can they explain it to you? Can they suggest ways that their difficulty might be made more manageable within the school setting?

- ADD/ADHD pupils need structure, so lists help. For example, be ready to hand out a list of the processes that are involved in writing an essay or how to behave when being told off (that can be of great help!).

- When a series of instructions need to be followed, it is likely that these will need to be presented more than once and in more than one way. Make sure you give these to the teaching assistant too, maybe as prompt cards or list cards.

- Eye contact is a good way of bringing a pupil back on task – using a supportive look, not a negative one.

- Seat the child near to your desk and make sure they are within your line of sight for most of the time. This will encourage them to stay on task. Give them a doodle pad too as this will help them to focus. I have also used adhesive tack, Koosh balls or stress balls in the past to help them relax.

- Use alternative methods of recording. Remember, what matters is that the child processes the information you impart. The method of processing can make a real difference to the child. Pen and paper is simple and convenient for the teacher, but if it doesn't work for the child then consider alternatives such as mind maps, graffiti boards, sticky note lists, audio equipment or note-taking on a digital device.

● Frequent feedback helps to keep ADD/ADHD pupils on task. It is also very useful for letting them know what is expected of them and if they are meeting expectations. This means simple, straightforward target-setting that is achievable. Naturally, praise will be very encouraging and, done well, helps to build intrinsic motivation – and we all need that!

● Break down larger tasks into smaller tasks or chunks. 'Chunk it' not 'clunk it' – if there is too much clunking then the child will get frustrated.

● Be humorous and have fun – anyone who laughs during learning is a happier and more motivated individual.

● Mind maps are brilliant so use them. Also try out some of the mind map apps or websites such as Popplet or SimpleMind+. Popplet has the advantage of allowing you to integrate text, images and handwriting too. What fun!

● Try to make tasks game orientated.

● Repeat, repeat and repeat in a calm way, so that ADD/ADHD children have a chance of remembering.

● The learning of older children will be enhanced considerably if they have a good idea in advance of what they will be learning that day. Here's your chance to integrate a bit of flipped and blended learning!

● Be on the lookout for things to enjoy about the child. For example, their energy and dynamism can be very beneficial for the group or class. Try to pick up on their talents and nurture these. As they have taken many of life's knocks, ADD/ADHD children tend to be resilient and are good at bouncing back, so they can be generous of spirit and always glad to help out.

 On page 204 there's a **RESOURCE** and some more **THINKING** for you.

STRATEGIES AND CONSIDERATIONS IN SUPPORTING LEARNERS WITH *ADD* AND *ADHD*

ORGANISATION OF LEARNING

- Use checklists
- Can find making previous learning connections difficult
- Forgetful with everyday tasks
- Create a visual timetable
- Support with photos, pictures and videos
- Use digital device to help plan and share learning – iPad is best
- Loses things very easily
- Use mind maps and visual learning tools

BEHAVIOUR

- Gets flustered completing tasks – needs support
- School work is not important
- Mistakes are plentiful
- Tasks rarely get completed – attention span a problem
- Keep tasks short and snappy
- Seems to be daydreaming and not listening
- Be kind and supportive when asking questions
- Difficulty focusing
- Chunk everything
- Will want to be heard sometimes and seen
- Can exhibit unusual, spur-of-the-moment behaviour

HYPERACTIVITY

- Fidgets a lot
- Loves to move, run, jump and climb
- Inappropriate physical movements at times
- Restless
- Needs to walk around classroom and can be noisy
- Likes to touch things
- May call out innapropriate comments

CONCENTRATION

- Can be sensitive to different sounds
- Sometimes will like music – the right music
- Difficulty in concentrating

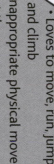
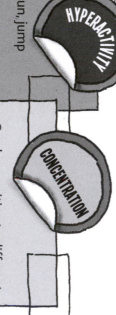

Resource from *Of Teaching, Learning and Sherbet Lemons* © Nina Jackson, Paul Wrangles, 20

31

THE DAUNTING DIFFICULTIES OF DYSPRAXIA

Q I HAVE A PUPIL IN MY CLASS WHO SEEMS TO BE CLUMSY ALL THE TIME – WALKING INTO THINGS, DROPPING THINGS, DISPLAYING VARIOUS COORDINATION PROBLEMS, THAT SORT OF THING. A COLLEAGUE SAID THEY MIGHT BE DYSPRAXIC. DOES THIS SOUND RIGHT?

A Before I get into the nitty-gritty of what dyspraxia is, my first tip is to keep a diary so you can monitor the difficulties the pupil seems to be having. If they have not been diagnosed with dyspraxia, so this is only a gut feeling from a well-meaning colleague, then at this stage it is important to ask for observations from a range of colleagues in school. Also ask the parents/carers if they have noticed any problems. The more people who can help the pupil to overcome any visible issues, such as clumsiness, that seem to be hampering their learning – as well as looking out for the emotional development of the child – the better it will be in the long run. We never want a child to feel there is something 'wrong' with them just because they can't always do the same things as other children of their age. Ensuring the child is emotionally well cared for is very important, as they may not know why it is that everyday things are not quite right and objects seem to just 'get in the way'.

A dyspraxic person can have problems in many areas, such as cognitive skills, physical movement and being unaware of their surroundings and objects close by, which, in turn, affect coordination, judgement and memory of where things are. Simply carrying a food tray in a school canteen can be a momentous task because holding the tray and negotiating their way to a seat is a difficult journey – finding the easiest route will be a real struggle. Many dyspraxics also have other medical problems as their immune system can be impaired.

Dyspraxia is a learning and living difference which is associated with motor-sensory issues. It used to be referred to as 'clumsy child syndrome' but is no longer (thankfully!). Eye, hand, foot coordination is really tricky, so dyspraxics struggle with everyday tasks like brushing their teeth and holding a knife and fork correctly. Many dyspraxic pupils get extremely anxious in physical education lessons or anything that involves catching or throwing a ball. They find computer games very difficult too because of coordination problems with using a hand-held controller.

Much like certain aspects of dyslexia, dyspraxics often have problems with thought processes and language development as well as sharing their thinking coherently. Planning anything will be a challenge because they find it hard to manage their thoughts. Organising and carrying out a plan will be just as complex for them, so dyspraxics need help with managing themselves as well as tasks and activities. Be sure to have some prompt cards or lists to support them in class and, in particular, for homework.

Dyspraxia does not affect a person's intelligence, although it can cause learning difficulties in children. Please note, then, that dyspraxia is not a disability. With the right intervention and support it is a condition that can be managed and supported well. Having a learning and living difference does not mean that there is a problem; it just means that the person needs more support than the average learner.

Daniel Radcliffe, star of the *Harry Potter* films, has dyspraxia and has described at length what it's like to live with it.[1] He's said that he went into acting partly because his dyspraxia meant he was not successful at school. Regarding tying shoelaces, he exclaimed, 'Why, oh why, has Velcro not taken off?' We all have talents – we just need to find the right avenue to channel these talents. Remember, it's that invisible stamp!

Hopefully this information might help you to understand some of the issues around dyspraxia and assist you in putting in place some simple steps to make sure your pupil feels safe and secure in the school environment. Please remember that referring to a child with a label can be detrimental to their progress, so always make reference to their first name – for example, 'Martin is a super thinker and very creative learner – we have to support him with his dyspraxic difficulties,' as opposed to 'Martin is dyspraxic.' The language the teacher uses is very important when it comes to developing a growth mindset, so be extra careful with children who are experiencing difficulties in this way. Always put the child first and the specific special educational need as an add-on to

---

1 See Emily Friedman, Dyspraxia Explains Harry Potter's Klutziness, *ABC News* (19 August 2008). Available at: http://abcnews.go.com/Health/story?id=5605093.

their identity rather than their entire identity. I have heard hundreds of educationalists over the years label children by their learning difference rather than calling them by their name. It's unforgiveable!

 Here are some of the signs and symptoms of dyspraxia to look out for and **THINK** about. Remember, some difficulties occur at particular developmental stages in a child's life.

- Basic physical developments such as sitting, crawling and walking – the Foundation for Dyspraxia suggests that many never go through the crawling stage.
- Speech and communication – often language development is slower and making sense of what words fit where is also an issue. Cognitive development can suffer and vocabulary is limited because it takes a long time to store new words.
- They will speak much slower than other children and often make noises rather than audible words.

Later on, the following difficulties may become apparent:

- Holding a knife and fork, tying shoe laces and holding a pen.
- Catching and kicking a ball, skipping, jumping and general outdoor games.
- Working with classroom objects such as paper and building blocks, cutting and using scissors, holding a jug and pouring water. They often find drawing and colouring a challenge.
- Difficulties with thought processing.
- Unable to focus well on tasks and can't remain on one job for too long.
- Unable to keep still for lengthy periods of time – they like to fidget (although fidgeting is good if lessons are boring!).
- Coordinating stairs or a short route around the playground is hard.
- Bumping into things is a common occurrence.
- Take longer to develop new learning and physical skills compared to other children.
- Copying anything down can cause severe anxiety as they find it hard to remember what they've read.
- Oral skills are better than written skills.

These symptoms are also common at pre-school age:

● Difficulty in making and keeping friends.

● Behaviour socially odd at times.

● Take more time to carry out tasks and activities and can seem a little hesitant.

● Gripping or holding and object is a challenge.

Later on in childhood you may see the following signs:

● Anxiety during sports or physical education lessons.

● Coping better with support or on a one-to-one basis.

● Written tasks are a challenge, in particular writing down numbers in maths.

● Either choose not to write or take a considerable length of time in writing simple words.

● Unable to follow instructions – they will give the impression that they are choosing not to follow instructions when in fact they find communication with the teacher quite difficult.

● Retention issues.

● Not well organised so forget many things.

Pupils with dyspraxia may be extremely sensitive to taste, light, touch and/or noise so it is good to be aware of their preferences. There may also be a lack of awareness of potential dangers. Many experience mood swings and display erratic behaviour. There can also be a tendency to take things literally.

 TRY some of these activities with dyspraxic pupils. There are hundreds to consider, so I have split them into those suitable for the main developmental ages.

PRE-SCHOOL/EARLY YEARS FOUNDATION STAGE

EATING AND DRINKING

Consider the type of cup the child is using. A soft cup is no good as they will squeeze it and not understand that it needs to be held softly. Choose a cup that is rigid and has a weighted base. A good-sized handle is important so the child can get all their fingers through the hole, giving them a better grip. The child should be sitting in a stable area or, if sitting on the floor, supported by a wall for extra stability. Do not ask them to carry the cup anywhere as this is likely to cause serious motor-sensory and coordination issues. Always take the child to the cup, and make sure it is not over-filled.

STORY TIME

Make story time as interactive as possible, using prompts to involve the child as they can get distracted easily. Large puppets and storybooks are brilliant. Give the child movement breaks and limit the amount of time on the floor. (I can't keep still for longer than a couple of minutes, so I imagine life for a child with dyspraxia can be hell!) If the child is unsettled or fidgeting, give them a fidget toy or Koosh ball (which is a pom-pom style ball made of soft rubber filaments, much like a stress ball – I do love a Koosh ball!) or even something from home to make them feel at ease. Engage the rest of the children in different sitting positions too, so the child does not feel they are being singled out for a special attention. Emotional well-being is as important as anything else.

PRIMARY SCHOOL

A TOOLKIT FOR THE CLASSROOM

Think about having the following easily achievable strategies in place for children with dyspraxia:

- Let the child choose from a toolbox of pens and pencils, ensuring the grip is the best one for them. They can then identify these as their 'magic writers'. We never want a child to feel different, so you could use this same method with all the children so they all have personalised learning tools.
- The shape of pens and the feel of rubbers and rulers is important. These will help with joint issues as the child becomes familiar with their texture and shape.
- Pencil sharpeners need to be stable desk-top types because a loose hand-held one will be difficult to manage.
- Angle boards are a great tool for supporting the child's arm, ensuring better writing and coordination.
- Positioning the child where they can hear and see well is vital.
- It's a good idea to put non-slip matting in place to stop books and equipment from moving and skidding around. You may also want to consider book rests and seating wedges.
- Always remember that the child's feet must be firmly placed on the floor when seated.

SECONDARY SCHOOL

Using ICT to support pupils with dyspraxia will be a great asset, not only because you are addressing every child's need to be a digital citizen but also because the integration of ICT into learning, task orientation and the development of fine motor skills is invaluable. ICT can get a child engaged in their learning, so holding a digital device becomes part of the physical, cognitive and emotional developmental process. I can particularly recommend iPads as there are so many apps that can support learning and life skills.

It's important that dyspraxic pupils begin typing as early as possible. Typequick touch-typing software is not only interactive but a great way of using games to promote learning too. Here's a link for you: www.typequick.co.uk/.

When using Microsoft Word, list commonly misspelled words in AutoCorrect – the program has built in word prediction software which can speed up typing and reduce spelling errors. You can also double click the 'Fn' button on a Mac to record speech. On an iPad, go to Settings > General > Accessibility > Speech Selection to set up the device to speak written text and decide how slow or fast highlighted text is spoken. If you have an updated iPad (iPad 4 onwards) you can use the microphone button on any text app – speak and it will type it for you. This is an ingenious way in which the thinking brain gets to work in partnership with the digital brain. If you want more help with using iPads with SEND children then please drop me a line.

 The **RESOURCE** on page 212 sets out some strategies that can help with dyspraxia.

 Here's another **RESOURCE** you may like. It's the Dyspraxia Foundation website which is excellent for resources and further help: www.dyspraxiafoundation.org.uk/.

CONSIDERATIONS FOR LEARNERS WITH *Dyspraxia*

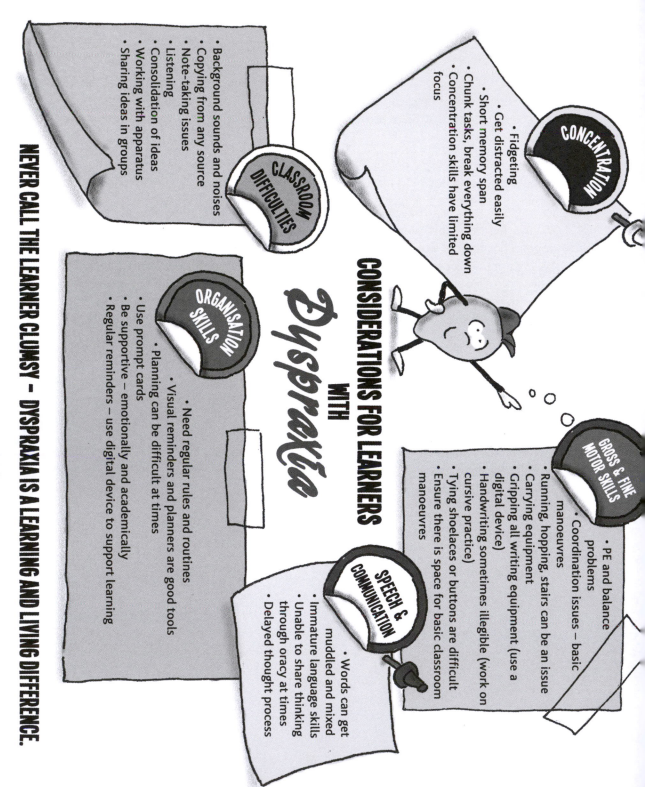

NEVER CALL THE LEARNER CLUMSY – DYSPRAXIA IS A LEARNING AND LIVING DIFFERENCE.

CONCENTRATION
- Fidgeting
- Get distracted easily
- Short memory span
- Chunk tasks, break everything down
- Concentration skills have limited focus

CLASSROOM DIFFICULTIES
- Background sounds and noises
- Copying from any source
- Note-taking issues
- Listening
- Consolidation of ideas
- Working with apparatus
- Sharing ideas in groups

ORGANISATION SKILLS
- Need regular rules and routines
- Visual reminders and planners are good tools
- Planning can be difficult at times
- Use prompt cards
- Be supportive – emotionally and academically
- Regular reminders – use digital device to support learning

GROSS & FINE MOTOR SKILLS
- PE and balance problems
- Coordination issues – basic manoeuvres
- Running, hopping, stairs can be an issue
- Carrying equipment
- Gripping all writing equipment (use a digital device)
- Handwriting sometimes illegible (work on cursive practice)
- Tying shoelaces or buttons are difficult
- Ensure there is space for basic classroom manoeuvres

SPEECH & COMMUNICATION
- Words can get muddled and mixed
- Immature language skills
- Unable to share thinking through oracy at times
- Delayed thought process

Resource from *Of Teaching, Learning and Sherbet Lemons* © Nina Jackson, Paul Wrangles, 20

32

DIGITAL LEADERS

Q I HAVE HEARD ABOUT DIGITAL LEADERS AND WOULD LIKE TO START THIS INITIATIVE IN MY SCHOOL, BUT I'M NOT SURE WHAT THEY REALLY ARE. DO YOU HAVE ANY ADVICE ABOUT WHETHER IT'S WORTHWHILE AND, IF IT IS, HOW I MIGHT DO THIS?

A While it's been said that the past is not what it was, the same can also be said of the future. I know it's a bit of a cliché to say that children are our future, but my mantra is: let's decide to be the best we can be because the children we teach are our future. These days, with all the amazingly rapid technological advances, the future seems to be whatever is just round the corner. So, if the future is to be bright, and more than just orange, we need to embrace change and innovation in an ever-evolving curriculum, especially when it comes to technology, And that counts from the early years to, well, as old as I am — if not *even* older!

Digital technology is now a part of nearly all our lives, whether we like or not. Even my 96-year-old grandfather (my tadcu) is aware of the remarkable world of technology, especially now he can send a text and see pictures of himself on the worldwide web. He is a man with no formal education, so imagine how magical all of this seems to him! What will we be amazed by when we are 96, I wonder?

For the children in our schools, smartphones, tablets and laptops are now a natural extension of their thinking. It's like having a third arm or what is called an 'outboard brain'! Digital devices are not an accessory any more, they have become an essential tool for 21st century learning and living — and it scares the living daylights out of some teachers and parents. If we are to move *with* our children, then we need to understand their needs and support them to operate in a digital world. But, and this is another important transformation, when it comes to technology, we can and should be learning from them too.

Digital leaders are young people who support others in the school from a learning technology perspective. They are enthusiastic about new technologies and take an active role in whole school ICT development in all areas of the curriculum. You can have digital leaders within a single class or they can work school wide as 'ambassadors'. Ultimately, it's about allowing children to lead on and share their knowledge, skills and understanding about the integral role that technology can play in the learning landscape.

So, developing digital leaders in your school is to be commended and congratulated. Whether you are ICT savvy yourself or not, it's about getting children to share their thinking and thirst for learning by integrating digital learning alongside other teaching and learning tools. Making changes and constantly evolving is what we do as teachers. Digital leaders can support transformational learning in the curriculum and encourage collaboration between teachers and their professional learning networks. Some schools run 'genius bars' for teachers at lunchtimes, with the students on hand to answer any questions about using digital devices and show teachers how to use simple collaboration and communication tools such as Padlet with other teachers.

Some digital leaders from primary schools are working not just with other pupils in their school, but also with their local community. A school in my area (the award-winning Casllwchwr Primary School in Swansea) has led the way in developing the Lifelong Intergenerational Furthering Education (LIFE) programme, through which pupils teach adults in their community to embrace technology as part of their everyday lives.[1]

 THINK about what digital leaders could do in your school. They could:

- Help to promote digital learning and technology across the school and within the curriculum to enhance the learning experience.
- Use their expertise to make lessons more fun, engaging and exciting for you and for pupils.
- Raise levels of attainment and achievement through an inclusive learning approach with technology.
- Ensure pupil voice is present across the school and in lessons, not just as part of a school or pupil council.

---

1   They have even won awards for it too – see: http://www.naace.co.uk/thirdmillenniumlearningaward/CasllwchwrPrimarySchool/.

● Promote pupil-led lessons and help to find different ways to show learner progress.

● Enhance children's learning through their passion for technology.

● Connect teachers more effectively with pupils in a non-threatening and collaborative learning environment.

● Encourage motivation through what I call 'digiplay' (learning through play is always best).

● Assist reluctant teachers to embrace technology in simple ways in lessons that would take advantage of what the pupils enjoy doing.

● Create multimedia opportunities for pupils and teachers.

● Improve pupil attendance and motivation for learning as well as attitudes, aspirations and behaviour – it might even improve staff morale too!

● Provide the more able and talented pupils with opportunities for extending and enriching their learning.

● Strengthen learning relationships between the digital leaders and teachers, and bring networked learning and collaboration to the forefront of curriculum delivery and development.

● Ensure that more learners are involved and are active participants and creative thinkers in lessons. Being a digital leader should become part of the daily school routine, embedded in the learning life of the school.

You may also find that the philosophy of the digital leaders has an effect on other departments. For example, you might start to have art ambassadors, pupil research champions or music masters, much like you may already have house captains linked to PE. Remember, being a digital leader should be a real honour. Pupils will aspire to reach new heights if they become a learning leader – and not just in the digital sense. The possibilities, if I may say so, are endless.

A little tip from me before you get going is to start small, but with a real belief in your idea and the power of student voice and collaboration. Remember too that one of the best things about digital leaders is that teachers can learn from them too. Tech-savvy children often have this in-built curiosity to find quirky and unusual ways of doing things (yes, you know it, we are all the same and yet we are all different!). We might all use the same tool, but by using it in different ways we open up many other questions and possibilities.

Now let's think about how you could begin to plan setting up the digital leaders initiative. **TRY** these ideas and take each step at a time:

1. Begin a marketing campaign to discover who your digital leaders might be. You could do this through assemblies, tutor time, year group meetings or even the school council. If you have a school Facebook or Twitter account then you could also advertise the initiative on social media. (Even better is to mention it to a pupil you already know is amazing with technology, then get them to publicise it by way of a taster as to what might lie ahead.)

2. Make it fair. Create an application system so the pupils have to apply to be a digital leader. Produce an online Google Docs application form – then you will know if they have the necessary know-how and determination. But also, to be fair and inclusive to socially disadvantaged or SEND pupils, create different versions on paper, for the iPad, with large text and/or different backgrounds.

3. Choose who you would like to interview based on their application. You may also want to suggest that they include an additional demonstration of their technological skills and expertise in the application process create a video application too. Think of the cross-curricular learning opportunities here – it's just like applying for a 'proper job'!

4. Ensure all staff are aware of your digital leaders programme and keep them informed via the staffroom notice board, group emails, Twitter or other social media.

5. When setting up your digital leaders initiative, ensure the pupils have a clear understanding of their roles and responsibilities. Create a 'policy to practice' document that outlines this and share it with governors, parents, staff and pupils in the school. Embrace everyone in this journey.

6. When creating your job description, you may want to include some of the following recommendations, as outlined by our friend and award-winning tech guru Mark Anderson (@ICTEvangelist). He suggests that you should:

   ◾ Ensure digital leaders are exemplary role models within the school and beyond, demonstrating good and safe use of technology.

- Support teachers with their use of apps for learning, as well as using them as collaborative tools with teachers.

- Be available and attend events that need digital leader input and support, such as parents' evenings, conferences, transition evenings, external speaker workshops, etc.

- Be available at a DigiArea, such as a DigiPod, DigiDesk or similar, in order to help other students with their digital questions and queries during lunchtimes and breaktimes.

- Run open drop-in DigiSessions so that pupils and staff can share ideas and be supported with their digital needs on an after-school or extra-curricular basis.

- Lead and run a school DigiMag to share with other pupils, staff and parents.

- Contribute at least one article per month to the DigiMag so that there is a consistent flow of new ideas.

You can also give digital leaders responsibility for certain online notifications, such as the effective and safe way of using Facebook and Twitter for learning and sharing essential information. They can set up great ways to share revision tips and tools as well. In this way, we can see blended learning in action!

I think it's time for you to embark on your own journey of discovery with digital technology for learning. Use digital leaders to create an ethos of shared practice, innovation and creativity in your school!

 There's a student digital leadership model **RESOURCE** on page 218.

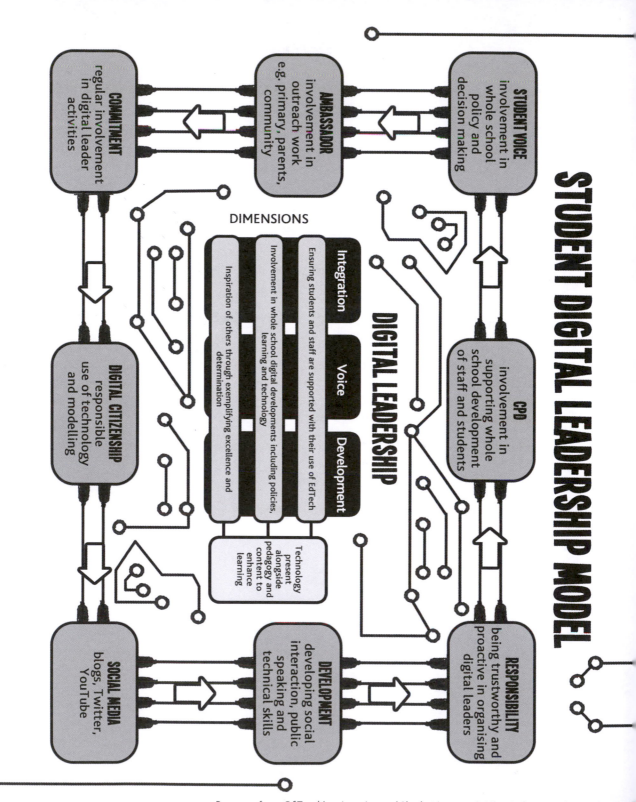

STUDENT DIGITAL LEADERSHIP MODEL

STUDENT VOICE
involvement in whole school policy and decision making

AMBASSADOR
involvement in outreach work e.g. primary, parents, community

COMMITMENT
regular involvement in digital leader activities

CPD
involvement in supporting whole school development of staff and students

DIGITAL CITIZENSHIP
responsible use of technology and modelling

RESPONSIBILITY
being trustworthy and proactive in organising digital leaders

SOCIAL MEDIA
blogs, Twitter, YouTube

DEVELOPMENT
developing social interaction, public speaking and technical skills

DIMENSIONS

DIGITAL LEADERSHIP

Integration
Ensuring students and staff are supported with their use of EdTech

Technology present alongside pedagogy and content to enhance learning

Voice
Involvement in whole school digital developments including policies, learning and technology

Development
Inspiration of others through exemplifying excellence and determination

Resource from *Of Teaching, Learning and Sherbet Lemons* © Nina Jackson, Paul Wrangles, 201

33

MY COLLEAGUES' BORING LESSONS!

Q I HAVE CHILDREN WHO ARE COMPLAINING ABOUT LESSONS WITH ANOTHER TEACHER IN MY SCHOOL. THEY TELL ME THEY ARE BORED, DON'T LEARN ANYTHING, THAT SHE ALWAYS TEACHES FROM THE FRONT AND THERE IS NEVER ANY REFERENCE TO THE USE OF DIGITAL LEARNING. THEY SAY THEY LEARN NOTHING! WHEN THEY ARRIVE IN MY LESSONS IT THEN TAKES ME A WHILE TO SETTLE THEM DOWN AS THEY JUST KEEP MOANING ABOUT THE TEACHER AND HER LESSONS. WHAT DO YOU SUGGEST, ESPECIALLY AS THE TEACHER CONCERNED IS A VERY DEAR FRIEND OF MINE AS WELL AS A PROFESSIONAL COLLEAGUE?

A The first thing we have to tackle is separating the professional from the personal. When we are in a professional role, regardless of our job, we have a duty to ourselves, our employers and our position to approach it with dedication and commitment and to do the best job we can. In this case, there's a duty towards the children and a duty towards the profession.

You are obviously torn between helping your friend, motivating the children you teach and ensuring there is minimum disruption at the beginning of your lesson. However, as you are in your place of professional work, it's essential that your professionalism comes first – that's what you're being paid for. Our professional obligations often require some thoughtful management, and being able to separate the personal from the professional is one of the most challenging.

While I'm a great believer in the maxim, 'work hard, play hard', it becomes very hard indeed if the work and the play overlap (i.e. when your colleague is also your friend). To maintain a professional working relationship we have to be able to disconnect one from the other. But how do we do it?

THINK about these two aspects of professionalism:

1. Personal relationships must not interfere with your professional judgement and duties. There's no choice to be made here: the professional obligation must always come first. It's your job and you have a position of trust with regards to your children.

2. Working or business relationships should be kept on a strictly professional basis. Professional standards in schools require absolute integrity at all times and in all areas of work. Conflicts of interest can seriously weaken your position in a working environment, so are best avoided as a matter of principle.

 So, with that line drawn in the sand, here are my tips for supporting your friend which (hopefully) bring together the professional and the personal. **TRY** these strategies:

● Tell your colleague that you want to develop some new ideas in your classroom and ask what ideas she has to share.

● Suggest creating a professional learning network and ask her to be a part of it to support you with new ideas. This will also be celebrated in your school as in-house CPD.

● Create a weekly focus such as:

   ■ How to assess learner progress over time, perhaps through learning journals or diaries. You might want to look at some online collaboration tools together, such as Padlet, BaiBoard or iBrainstorm, so that she can use these with her students. This will help with that missing digital learning element which the children mentioned to you.

   ■ Motivational learning tools – using music, visualisation, games, questioning, BYOD for learning, digital collaboration, etc.

   ■ Assessment through feedback – developing a culture of dialogue and target-setting from a personal relationship angle with the children, making sure every individual matters.

And so on … If I start now and share all my suggestions with you we will be here until next year! Hopefully you get the idea. Sit and brainstorm with your colleague – remember, your best resource in school is each other.

Developing a culture of openness and dialogue about learning for your children and yourselves is crucial in the ever-changing world of education. Here are some more ideas to **TRY**:

- Set up a Twitter account for professional dialogue. Get her engaged in educational chat and show her that she can access amazing learning blogs and free resources online.

- Be brave enough to tell her about the issues pupils have with 'another' teacher (who shall remain nameless!). Then ask her what she would suggest as ways of helping this teacher to refocus the learners. Often, when someone is given the responsibility to rise to a challenge, you will be surprised by their response.

- Try out the same ideas together in different classes and lessons and report back to each other on what worked and what didn't. Often, the same idea can work brilliantly with some classes but fall flat with others. It's about meeting the needs of the learners and giving them different learning experiences from an inclusive and differentiated angle, which is what every teacher should be doing!

- If you are a strong personality and you feel your colleague won't be personally hurt, then tell her how it is!

Whatever strategy you decide to go for, just remember that you are doing yourself and the children a professional courtesy by working to make things better. You are also performing a personal courtesy by supporting your friend in a non-threatening and collaborative way, which will serve to improve things for all concerned.

But what do you do if none of this has any impact? As professionals, we all know that we have a duty to reach and maintain certain standards and, as teachers, we need to show that learners can make progress over time. If this is an issue, and learners are not making progress, then the teacher's line manager must take responsibility for addressing the issue in the first instance.

Over a period of time, through observations, discussions, meetings, target-setting and taking accountability for her professional impact on learning, if standards of teaching and learning are still not met then the line manager will have no option but to refer your colleague to senior management. This means she will have a formal plan set out for her. If there is any doubt about whether she is able to fulfil her duties then appropriate action will have to be taken.

If your colleague has lost her spark and enthusiasm for teaching, and her heart isn't in it any more, then a good friend would suggest an alternative career or job. Depending on her age, she might even want to take early retirement. The worst thing for any school is to have teachers who are burnt out and running on empty. It doesn't do the profession, the learning, the school or the teacher any favours for them to carry on. Teaching is a profession we should feel proud of, so we should not endorse schools holding on to ineffectual, inadequate teachers.

The **RESOURCE** on page 223 might help.

Why Professional Learning Networks are full of FIZZ!

They provide a platform from which to articulate and communicate the school's mission, vision and goals to all community members (parents, governors, teachers and staff)

They create opportunities for shared leadership by serving as a schoolwide depository to which all stakeholders may contribute and from which they may also benefit

They ensure opportunities for all voices to be heard by building participatory forums

They deliver differentiated professional development for collective and individual learning and instruction

They celebrate shared practices by housing and making available model lessons, presentations and student products to all teachers

They provide space for posting student data, publishing school initiatives and collaborating with colleagues to determine best teaching practices with regard to common curriculum expectations

Resource from *Of Teaching, Learning and Sherbet Lemons* © Nina Jackson, Paul Wrangles, 2015

EPILOGUE

So, there you have it.

It's been a bit of a journey with the amazing, sensitive and difficult questions that teachers want and need to ask to get the teaching and learning right. It's been a full jar of sherbet lemons all along the way, and the spectrum of questions asked has been huge. But it's not about the hugeness of anything – it's about getting that misplaced sherbet back into those lemons!

I hope this book will help all teachers with their personal quest of finding and putting the fizz back into everything they do. Your questions have already fired my own Ninja thinking, which is as much about professional rigour and standards as it is the magical sherbet experience. Great teaching makes me feel all fizzy inside.

Right … I'm off to buy a new jar of sherbet lemons, and I shall keep some spare in case any of you need one now and then.

So, to conclude: if you ever have a sherbet lemon that has lost its zing or is missing its sherbet because it's one of the 'dodgy' ones, then do get in touch and I'd be more than happy to help.

Here are my details:

@musicmind

tlcninajackson@gmail.com

teachlearncreate.com

Nina

x

BIBLIOGRAPHY

Acosta, Simone and Richards, Regina G. (1999). Cursive Writing: A Multisensory Approach. In California Consortium, *Resource Directory* (Baltimore, MD: International Dyslexia Association).

American Psychiatric Association (2013). *Diagnostic and Statistical Manual of Mental Disorders, Fifth Edition (DSM-5)* (Arlington, VA: APA).

Anderson, Mark (2013). *Perfect ICT Every Lesson* (Carmarthen: Independent Thinking Press).

Beere, Jackie (2011). *The Perfect Ofsted Lesson* (Carmarthen: Crown House Publishing).

Beukeboom, Camiel J., Tanis, Martin and Vermeulen, Ivar E. (2013). The Language of Extraversion: Extraverted People Talk More Abstractly, Introverts Are More Concrete, *Journal of Language and Social Psychology* 32(2): 191–201.

Blatchford, Peter, Baines, Ed, Rubie-Davies, Christine, Bassett, Paul and Chowne, Anne (2006). The Effect of a New Approach to Group-Work on Pupil–Pupil and Teacher–Pupil Interaction, *Journal of Educational Psychology* 98 (2006): 750–765.

Boseley, Sarah (2011). Self-Harm Practised By One In 12 Adolescents, Study Reveals, *The Guardian* (17 November). Available at: http://www.theguardian.com/society/2011/nov/17/self-harm-in-adolescents-study/.

Cohen, Louis, Manion, Lawrence and Morrison, Keith (2011). *Research Methods in Education*, 7th edn (Abingdon: Routledge).

Davies, Ronald D. and Braun, Eldon M. (2010). *The Gift of Dyslexia: Why Some of the Brightest People Can't Read and How They Can Learn* (New York: J. P. Tarcher/Penguin Putnam).

Edwards, Anna (2013). 'Epidemic' of Children As Young As Five Self-Harming Warns Charity, *Daily Mail* (5 February). Available at: http://www.dailymail.co.uk/news/article-2273638/Epidemic-children-young-self-harming-warns-charity.html/.

Friedman, Emily (2008). Dyspraxia Explains Harry Potter's Klutziness, *ABC News* (19 August). Available at: http://abcnews.go.com/Health/story?id=5605093.

Gilbert, Ian (2006). *The Big Book of Independent Thinking: Do Things No One Does or Do Things Everyone Does In a Way No One Does* (Carmarthen: Crown House Publishing).

Gilbert, Ian (2012). *Essential Motivation in the Classroom*, 2nd edn (Abingdon: Routledge).

Gilbert, Ian, Gilbert, William, Gilbert, Olivia and Gilbert, Phoebe (2010). *The Little Book of Bereavement for Schools* (Carmarthen: Crown House Publishing).

Glennie, Alasdair (2014). Pushy Parents 'Stressing Pupils': Expert Says Growing Number of Children Are Risking Their Mental Health Because They Are So Terrified of Getting Bad Results, *Daily Mail* (22 May). Available at: http://www.dailymail.co.uk/news/article-2635736/Pushy-parents-stressing-pupils-Expert-says-growing-number-pupils-risking-mental-health-pressure-deliver-grades.html/.

Goddard, Vic (2014). *The Best Job in the World* (Carmarthen: Independent Thinking Press).

Hill, Amelia (2008). Even 5-Year-Olds Are At Risk from Self-Harm, Parents Are Warned, *The Guardian* (3 August). Available at: http://www.theguardian.com/society/2008/aug/03/mentalhealth.children/.

Jackson, Nina (2009). *The Little Book of Music for the Classroom: Using Music to Improve Memory, Motivation, Learning and Creativity* (Carmarthen: Crown House Publishing).

Moon, Sidney (n.d.). Extraordinary Lives and Difficult Goals, *Center for Talent Development, School of Education and Social Policy, Northwestern University*. Available at: http://www.ctd.northwestern.edu/resources/displayArticle/?id=141/.

O'Dolan, Catherine (2010). Why Children Love Secret Hiding Places, *Baby and Toddler* (6 August). Available at: http://www.juniormagazine.co.uk/baby-and-toddler/why-children-love-secret-hiding-places/2473.html/.

Ofsted (2000). *Evaluating Educational Inclusion: Guidance for Inspectors and Schools* (London: Ofsted).

Ostrander, Shelia, Schroeder, Lynn and Ostrander, Nancy (1994). *Super Learning 2000* (New York: Delacorte Press).

Paton, Graeme (2013). Three-Year-Olds 'Coached to Get Into Top Private Schools', *Daily Telegraph* (11 February). Available at: http://www.telegraph.co.uk/education/educationnews/9860555/Three-year-olds-coached-to-get-into-top-private-schools.html/.

PricewaterhouseCoopers LLP (2007). *Independent Study into School Leadership* (January). Ref: RB818. Available at: http://webarchive.nationalarchives.gov.uk/20130401151715/http://www.education.gov.uk/publications/eOrderingDownload/RB818.pdf.

Rashid, Nargis (2010). *Inclusion and Diversity in Education: Guidelines for Inclusion and Diversity in Schools* (Madrid: British Council).

Roberts, Hywel (2012). *Oops! Helping Children Learn Accidentally* (Carmarthen: Independent Thinking Press).

Ryan, Will (2008). *Leadership with a Moral Purpose: Turning Your School Inside Out* (Carmarthen: Crown House Publishing).

Smith, Jim (2010). *The Lazy Teacher's Handbook: How Your Students Learn More When You Teach Less* (Carmarthen: Crown House Publishing).

Sparky Teaching (2014). *365 Things To Make You Go Hmmm …* (Carmarthen: Independent Thinking Press).

Telegraph, The (2011). GCSEs: Pressure of Exams Leaves Teens Suffering from Mental Illness (25 August). Available at: http://www.telegraph.co.uk/education/educationnews/8720513/GCSEs-Pressure-of-exams-leaves-teens-suffering-from-mental-illness.html/.

Vasagar, Jeevan (2012). Me, Miss! Why Blurting Out the Answers Can Be Good for Pupils, *The Guardian* (2 February). Available at: http://www.theguardian.com/education/2012/feb/02/blurting-out-answers-good-for-pupils/.